The City That Is Leaving Forever

ALSO BY RAHAT KURD

Cosmophilia

published by Talonbooks

The City That
Is Leaving Forever

Kashmiri Letters

Rahat Kurd
&
Sumayya Syed

Talonbooks

Talonbooks
9259 Shaughnessy Street, Vancouver, British Columbia, Canada V6P 6R4
talonbooks.com

Talonbooks is located on xʷməθkʷəy̓əm, Sḵwx̱wú7mesh, and səl̓ilwətaʔɬ Lands.

First printing: 2021

Typeset in Minion
Printed and bound in Canada on 100% post-consumer recycled paper

Cover design and illustration by andrea bennett. Interior by Typesmith.

Talonbooks acknowledges the financial support of the Canada Council for the Arts, the Government of Canada through the Canada Book Fund, and the Province of British Columbia through the British Columbia Arts Council and the Book Publishing Tax Credit.

LIBRARY AND ARCHIVES CANADA CATALOGUING IN PUBLICATION

Title: The city that is leaving forever : Kashmiri letters / Rahat Kurd and
    Sumayya Syed.
Names: Kurd, Rahat, author. | Syed, Sumayya, author.
Identifiers: Canadiana 20210176253 | ISBN 9781772013573 (softcover)
Subjects: LCSH: Kurd, Rahat—Correspondence. | LCSH: Syed,
    Sumayya—Correspondence. | LCSH: Poets, Kashmiri—British
    Columbia—Correspondence. | LCSH: Poets, Kashmiri—India—
    Jammu and Kashmir—Correspondence. | LCSH: Women—British
    Columbia—Social conditions. | LCSH: Women—India—Jammu and
    Kashmir—Social conditions. | LCSH: Instant messaging. | LCSH:
    Jammu and Kashmir (India)—Social conditions. | CSH: Poets,
    Canadian (English)—British Columbia—Correspondence. | LCGFT:
    Personal correspondence.
Classification: LCC PS8621.U73 Z48 2021 | DDC C811/.6—dc23

For Aijaz and Ayaan, and for the poets of
Kashmir, past, present, and future

Contents

The City That Is Leaving Forever

List of Poems by Rahat Kurd

List of Poems by Sumayya Syed

Preface

In March 2012, visiting UBC from Berkeley, California, the Kashmiri American academic activist Huma Dar threw questions about Kashmir's political history out to the audience at her presentation and discussion of Sanjay Kak's 2007 film, *Jashn-e-Azadi*. Sitting near the front, not knowing anyone else in attendance – friends had sent me the event details only that morning, urging me to go and meet her (South Asians do make it a point of pride, I find, to try to connect their Kashmiris) – I knew many of the answers by heart, and I raised my hand. So did one other person in the audience, whom I could hear, but not see. Amused, Huma clearly surmised that she had found the other Kashmiris in the room, calling on us by turns and weaving our responses into her talk. We sought each other out for introductions as soon as the presentation ended, and that is how I met Sumayya Syed.

When Sumayya told me that she had been born in the same city as my mother, her mention of Srinagar opened a portal, an immediate understanding of home between strangers, making possible the kind of conversation I'd never before had with anyone who lived in Vancouver.

The shared endeavour of this book, emerging from unexpected circumstances and kept up for five years, was preceded in my case by several decades of living as though it were completely normal never to speak about Kashmir to anyone outside my mother's family; to carry my memories and hopes of returning there mostly in silence; and to come quite late to the necessity of writing about it. I had either made up, or – from the North American discursive environment that initially formed me as a writer – obeyed some rule in which Kashmir's invisibility was an established fact, puzzled over but never seriously confronted.

This was an entirely manufactured invisibility. India sent hundreds of thousands of its armed forces to occupy Kashmir before the global digital revolution, so that the simpler technologies of communication we relied on since my childhood – handwritten letters only rarely supplemented by international phone calls – persisted long past their obsolescence elsewhere. In our Canadian quotidian, receiving an airmail letter from my aunts and cousins always constituted an exciting event; photographs and parcels were exceptionally rare and wonderful. When long-distance calls became more affordable in the early 1990s, our connection to family in Kashmir was frequently constrained by the suspension of mail delivery, communication blackouts, travel restrictions, and banned news coverage long before the existence of cellular phone towers and the internet provided a succession of Indian regimes with new technologies of blockade and repression.

Meanwhile, in the artistic and literary circles of Vancouver, I found a particularly blithe twenty-first-century insistence on representing India generally as a source of feel-good cultural heritage, celebratory food, and non-stop dance-party aesthetics. This (admitted improvement over the vicious anti-Asian racism I witnessed growing up) left me little space, except within smaller activist contexts, to address the increasingly strident militarism of the world's largest democracy. And I found myself reluctant to take on the role of Kashmir Explainer, even when the people sensitive to the occupation in those contexts invited me to do so. Indeed until I was finally able to return to Kashmir in 1998, I remained as much at a loss to piece together what the occupation meant for my family, our friends, and for Kashmiri society and futures as any outsider. Until I began to make a way through writing poems, it was especially slow work to find ways to describe whatever I did know about Kashmir – crucially, without reproducing narratives of total defeat and flattening hopelessness.

Competing impulses of mine have propelled this book from its earliest development through to its publication. The first, towards writing-as-being, writing as an affirmation of daily life, however unfinished and full of struggle it may feel – a feminist affirmation of creative necessity in the midst of loss and destruction, and one that trusts the reader to put the pieces together – dwells in tension with my sense of duty to assess, contextualize, and account for the multiple factors that have brought us all here, to make an effort to bring order, legibility, and linear cohesion to seeming chaos.

That feeling of duty arises from my consciousness of the silencing and invisibilizing forces of occupation, the lengths of my absence, and my failure to learn Koshur (or Kashmiri), and how these have inhibited my previous efforts to write about Kashmir. It is vital to mark the ways in which that silencing has come to a definitive and resounding end – not solely because when the Modi-Shah regime nullified all autonomous Kashmiri legal structures, annexing the land as a centrally controlled "union territory" in August 2019, the world's news platforms gave the event unprecedented attention and urgency – but because Kashmiri voices of resistance have grown in strength and assuredness in response, calling for solidarity, accountability, and justice.

Kashmiri men and women are patiently mapping new lines of resistance and building global solidarity with their writing and activism. Journalists persist with innovative reporting on the ground in the face of repression, under threat of imprisonment. Poets and musicians are reviving old forms to create new art. Scholars and activists are researching, teaching, and translating Kashmiri literature, culture, and histories, and advocating staunchly against hopelessness, against rigid legal and discursive structures that seek to normalize land theft, religious apartheid, and militarized violence, for the sake of a life-giving future. Sumayya and I felt able to persist with this unconventional work, an effort by two poets to name the things that can survive erasure, because of their courage.

—Rahat Kurd

How to read The City That is Leaving Forever

2021-08-23

Text messages written by Sumayya F. Syed are preceded
by a dotted vertical line and are flush left. 1:47 PM

Text messages written by Rahat Kurd are preceded by a
solid vertical line and are indented from the left. 1:48 PM

Poems

Are preceded by a gray solid line
indented from the left
spaced between Rahat's and Sumayya's text
using a slightly smaller font
1:50 PM

Descriptions of links originally included in the authors' WhatsApp
correspondence, as well as descriptions of photographs that have been
omitted (either for reasons of permission or of quality) are preceded by
a gray hashed line indented from the left and spaced between Rahat's and
Sumayya's text, also in a slightly smaller font. 1:55 PM

Note on Orthography

Variations in the spelling of words transliterated from languages such
as Urdu and Arabic have been retained in the following exchange as an
acknowledgment of the difficulties inherent in translation and transliter-
ation and to preserve the informal nature and orthography of the original
WhatsApp exchanges.

Prologue

This Saturday or Sunday?

Rahat Kurd
Tues., Oct. 28, 2014, 11:46 PM

To: Sumayya F. Syed ▼

Dear Sumayya,

The weather is unlovely and the days are dark, but my friend Anjum is coming again this Saturday. Would you like to join us? She will be staying with me overnight and going to North Van for her course on Sunday. We could sit by my fireplace on Saturday night, or have breakfast on Sunday – or both. You are welcome to stay here overnight, too (if F. can spare you).

I don't know if you have time to take on extra reading, but I am sending you the poems I finished writing last June – this is a series called "Seven Stones for Jamarat." I am waiting to hear from the literary journal – they are supposed to be published soon – but, in the meantime, I hope you enjoy them. (Please don't share the electronic file with anyone – you may print the poems and delete the file.)

Salam and hope to see you again soon,

Rahat

New Year Salam

Sumayya F. Syed
Sunday, January 4, 2015, 11:50 PM

To: Rahat Kurd ▼

Dear Rahat,

I hope you have been well.

I am sorry I haven't been able to stay in touch. I had to leave Vancouver in kind of a rush and wasn't able to say goodbye. Please forgive me for this. I hope we can meet sometime when you're visiting Kashmir, inshallah.

Kashmir is desolate after the flood. The winter is terribly cold, but, as usual, the people are warm.

Wishing you the best in the new year,

Sumayya

PART ONE

Curfew for Beginners

Kismat Hamara Kya Cheez Hai.

Was supposed to be somewhere over the Atlantic
tonight, on an epic YVR > DEL > SXR with my kid,
if it weren't for war and occupation. If the Indian
military had to sell organic samosas stuffed with veggies
grown by happy land-/soil-/water-/seed-/food-secure
farmers to raise money to build its bunkers, for every
one of which it had to beg permission and design tips
from local teams of six-year-olds, if each bullet cost a
million dollars and twelve weeks of paperwork, if every
"live kill" of a Kashmiri civilian earned a hundred
Angry Aunty "YOU'RE NOT BEING THE CHANGE,
BESHARAM" slaps, not War on Terror performance
points, I would be free to wander around and write
poems about Kashmiri saffron. Not with shadows of
fighter jets passing over them on the way to the LOC,
no combat boots trampling them into oblivion. They
would just be intensely boring poems about Kashmiri
saffron, quietly growing. You would all beg me to stop.
"Please, not again with the saffron, doesn't Kashmir
have any other spices?" I would smile. I would say no.

Salam Rahat, I hope you've arrived safe and well. 4:20 PM

Just managed an internet connection. Please
let me know how I can contact you in Srinagar
while the world is shut on us. 4:20 PM

RAHAT KURD

Dear Sumayya, I was forced to cancel my trip. I am still
in shock. On Friday the eighth, I went to an Eid dinner
party and told everyone I was leaving in one week. I felt
really happy. The next morning, I woke up to the news
about Burhan Wani and curfews and pellet guns. And

an email from Aijaz's father asking if the curfew would be lifted and, if not, he didn't want Aijaz to go. And then followed many frantic conversations with my mother and my aunt. Between four of us adult family members and with the siege continuing through the week, we decided to cancel our tickets. This morning, I would have woken up in Srinagar. This is the only thought I seem to be able to hold in my head. How are you? Please tell me what I can do while the world is shut on you. 2:13 PM

2016-07-19

Rahat, amid all the pain, it's even harder to process that you're not visiting this summer. Perhaps Allah has better plans. We'll meet in happier times, inshallah. On the seventeenth I was excited and couldn't stop telling my parents that you were here and that I had to find a way to reach you. I am all right, as one can be in these circumstances. Not being able to leave the house takes its toll on the mind. It's more a curfew of the mind. But I do have good news. :) Which I was hoping to share with you in person. I got engaged around Eid. 11:06 AM

Although the terror of marriage still haunts me, I decided to not entrust my complete existence to a single point of affection. My family has been incredibly supportive through my darkest days, and I am hopeful of finding strength in their love in the days to come. Nevertheless, the prospect of being in a relationship still terrifies me. 11:06 AM

2016-07-20

Oh God, Sumayya. Can you believe this fate – planning for so long, then this non-arrival. I am in such a suspended state. I want to write. People here are incredibly ignorant about Kashmir. I feel so stricken at the thought of how you and our family were waiting for us. What do you do in the house? Do you read, write? Talk? I keep seeing our house, the brick walls, the garden and the streets ... Whom will you be marrying? When I heard about the curfews, I wondered about the summer wedding season ... Your engagement is happy news and yet you speak of dark days, pain, and terror. 9:48 PM

I hope your path grows lighter and
filled with ease. 9:48 PM

Did you ever receive my book? I had it posted
from Delhi in early February ... 10:42 PM

2016-07-21

No, I did not receive the book; sadly things often get lost
in the Indian postal system. The curfew is mental more
than anything, and it has managed to reach you all the
way to Vancouver, which is the real terror of it. 11:50 AM

I am happy about the engagement, alhamdulillāh. On
the conscious level, it seems to be the right thing to
do. I just feel that I may not be ready for another loss,
and I feel vulnerable to loss. A. works here in Srinagar
and his family lives not far from my parents' house.
And that is a blessing. He is also a caring person,
although our interests do not overlap much. 11:50 AM

Ah, so you will continue to make your life in
Srinagar – that makes me happy. 6:43 PM

2016-08-14

How are you, dear Sumayya? How is life in Srinagar, what
can you tell me? I am back in Vancouver now. I went to
Los Angeles with Aijaz. Stayed with Anjum whom you
met at my place in Vancouver. Our sons became friends.
Her garden has a lime tree and the air smelled like mint
and flowers. We met another Kashmiri friend of our youth
as well. It was a rich, brief time of rare happiness. 1:01 PM

2016-08-18

Salam Rahat, I am happy to know you have been having
a quietly nice summer. Things aren't good in Srinagar or
anywhere else in Kashmir. Broadband internet service just
resumed in Srinagar. Otherwise there was complete blackout.
The situation is worsening as they're killing more and
more people and putting on more restrictions ... 3:56 PM

There are restrictions on movement and speech and
light and sound and smell. It's almost autumn and

the beauty of early autumn is almost cruel in its
intensity. Everyone is incredibly frustrated. 3:56 PM

The zeitgeist isn't of revolution but of wretchedness. 3:56 PM

Yes. Thank you for putting it into words. 11:29 AM

2016-08-21

Just found this article on Twitter. Exactly
what I needed. I hope you have a chance to
read it. Sending love and strength.

Link to an article by Chinki Sinha, "Everyone's a poet of loss, memory,
and madness in Kashmir," *Daily O*, August 17, 2016. 12:18 PM

2016-08-26

Have you composed any poems, Sumayya? Please
send me a few if you can. I hope I am not burdening
you or being tiresome. Since I couldn't come, I
just have to try to do something. 12:29 PM

Rahat, please forgive me for my tardiness in responding.
I have been feeling a little overwhelmed with everything
lately and find myself withdrawing. I can imagine how it
must feel not to have been able to visit Kashmir, and then
to witness news of such daily hopelessness. The only way
to describe what I experience here is the clash of extreme
force and extreme resistance. I am personally devoid of
any hope. But every time someone leaves their house,
they seem do so with the resolve to return with azadi,
even if they're just going out looking for bread. 9:08 AM

*Freedom/
liberty. In
Persian and
other
language*

Unfortunately, I haven't been able to compose poems, I am
too overwhelmed. From the ground, resistance seems very
tiresome and it is easiest to give in. But this is a long, long
curfew, and people are in no mood to give in. 9:08 AM

2016-08-28

Thank you for writing. When you say you find yourself
withdrawing, I can easily imagine the effect it would
have on me to be in the situation you describe. I feel
stunned by the injustice of this situation. One of my

aunts suffers from depression. My cousins are very
harshly critical of Kashmiri society after all they
have lived through, but it's very rare that we get the
chance to talk about things in depth. Please keep on
writing to me whenever you want. And on any subject.
I wish my book had gotten to you, at least. 9:40 AM

Inshallah I will. It helps me to articulate what I experience;
that is probably the only way to live in a state of mental and
emotional curfew. I have actually ordered your book from
Amazon. ☺ It's stuck at the post office, though, and it'll get
to me as soon as things get moving, inshallah. 10:13 PM

I am grateful to you for writing. Although I wish
you had been here, even if it was a situation of siege,
I also feel glad that you stayed out and escaped this
curfew that sticks like tar to your eyelids. At least
some of us need to be out and voice us. 10:13 PM

2016-09-01

How are things today, Sumayya? 9:14 AM

Bleak. 9:46 PM

Yes. Nothing good in the news, either. 11:39 AM

2016-09-18

The prolonged darkness messes with your head. 8:03 AM

I will send you some lines / stanzas soon, inshallah. 8:04 AM

Sending you what love is possible from
a place of despair. 8:05 AM

And grateful for all the love you have been sending. 8:05 AM

2016-09-17

Dear Sumayya, I realize the communication delays are
not in your control. I can well imagine that being in that
darkness would mess with my head too. I am so grateful
you are all at least physically all right & grateful too for
the powerful things you have already said to me. 10:58 PM

2016-09-20

> Dear Sumayya, how are things? Are you
> able to go out these days? 7:05 AM

Salam, no. It is extremely difficult to get out of
the house. To restock supplies. 7:35 PM

> 😢 And schools and shops – closed? 7:40 AM

Schools have been closed all these months. 8:15 PM

Shops too. 8:15 PM

My niece and nephew have missed an
entire academic year. 8:15 PM

> How do they cope with being at home every
> day? How are their spirits? 7:47 AM

They end up being extremely cranky. 8:18 PM,

My four-year-old niece hates Mehbooba Mufti. 8:18 PM

Who has become her single locus of the curfew. 8:18 PM

*Indian politician 9th ? last chief minister of Jammu ? Kashmir

At every mealtime she likes to share with me
new ideas of how she's going to fool the soldiers
and get out of the curfew. 8:19 PM

> Oh my God, that a four-year-old's mind must bend
> itself around political oppression! 7:50 AM

On Eid I took her out with me to Eid prayer. 8:20 PM

And there were soldiers everywhere. 8:20 PM

She kept asking me why they were not shooting at us. 8:20 PM

I couldn't find an answer. 8:21 PM

So finally I told her it was because they were
scared of a girl like her. 8:21 PM

And she has been very proud since then. 8:21 PM

She offers to accompany her Babajan when he
wants to go looking for groceries. 8:22 PM

Because her presence will deter the soldiers. 8:22 PM

☺ 7:52 AM

May she always walk in that confidence & strength. 7:53 AM

And may no miscreant ever dare to contradict her. 7:54 AM

Ameen. 8:24 PM

Where was the Eid Gah in relation to your house? 7:54 AM

How long was the walk? 7:54 AM

A few blocks away. 8:25 PM

But they had dispatched the army. 8:25 PM

Were there armed soldiers in the prayer area? 7:59 AM

Yes. 8:29 PM

And lining the streets. 8:29 PM

Everywhere. 8:29 PM

From my house to the mosque. 8:29 PM

I suppose telling you where to go and how to go. 8:00 AM

Standing outside every door. 8:30 PM

They were quiet, didn't say or do anything. Some were even having breakfast out of tiffins. 8:30 PM

And the masjids were roaring with takbeer. 8:31 PM

Oh, I see. 8:01 AM

They were benevolently allowing the ritual to go on? 8:03 AM

I think they were a little overawed by the spirit, even though there was no festivity. 8:34 PM

It was like they couldn't decide what to think. 8:34 PM

But there was no mistaking their intention, with guns pointing in the right direction. 8:34 PM

Fingers ready. 8:34 PM

One soldier actually looked away when my niece and I walked by, she in her full Eid gear with Pakistani shalwar suit and matching earrings. 😄 8:35 PM

And she didn't fail to notice that. 8:36 PM

She said, "He's whispering to the other soldier to not try anything." 8:36 PM

> Oh my God. 8:17 AM
>
> I bet she reminded him of someone in his own family. 8:18 AM

Very likely. 8:48 PM

> It's an incredible image. 8:19 AM
>
> Just in words. 8:20 AM
>
> Almost more so than any photo would be. 8:20 AM

😄 Although I do wish I could have taken a photo. Her in her glamorous Eid outfit and newfound power, and them in their miserable tired uniforms. 8:51 PM

> Yes. It's brilliant from every angle. 8:22 AM

She actually spent the rest of the day narrating the incident to anyone who would listen. 8:52 PM

> What about you – what did the Eid prayer mean for you? What can it mean under the soldiers' eyes and guns? 8:24 AM

It was a continuation of mental and spiritual exhaustion. The khutbah was extremely demoralizing. 8:55 PM

Very patriarchal, and the khateeb did not make a single reference to the occupation or the brutality. It was so disconnected from reality. Harping on about how obedient Ibrahim's wife was to him. 8:55 PM

> Oh ewwwww! 8:26 AM

So many layers of exhaustion. 8:56 PM

> Absolutely. Clearly out of ideas, 8:27 AM
>
> Should I presume it was basically a CM-approved and state-mandated khutba? 8:28 AM

Well, this mosque / organization is known to toe a very "safe" line vis-à-vis resistance. 8:59 PM

They're known to openly denounce the resistance as un-Islamic. But it was the only masjid that would accommodate women. And relatively safe to walk to on such a morning. So I went there. 8:59 PM

> Thank you so much for recounting all of this to me. So vividly. I can imagine myself in your shoes. 8:31 AM
>
> When I stayed with Anjum, she just recounted a brief instance of the stubborn arrogance of men towards women – I think it was in her father's family or village. 8:34 AM
>
> It must get a lot worse at times like this? 8:34 AM

I have seen it go both ways. 9:05 PM

These are times when women take the foreground simply because it is unsafe to be a man. 9:06 PM

A young man. 9:06 PM

Who is seen as the most imminent form of danger to the state. Because of patriarchal assumptions of women being inherently less dangerous. 9:07 PM

But the men are also grateful for this cover. 😃 9:08 PM

> Ha ha, well … 8:38 AM
>
> I'm glad they appreciate it. 8:38 AM

So, in a way, my niece's offer to accompany her father to provide safety isn't that unfounded. 9:08 PM

Men can't go out alone. 9:08 PM

They prefer to take a woman or child with them. 9:09 PM

> It's profound. 8:39 AM

My brother actually had a narrow escape. 9:09 PM

The army men lunged at him in the dark as he was on his bike. 9:09 PM

And he screamed that he had kids with him. 9:10 PM

And they let him go. 9:10 PM

> Oh how terrible! 8:40 AM
>
> How terrible this is! 8:40 AM
>
> Thank God he is all right. 8:41 AM
>
> But at what terrible cost to you all. To the children. 8:41 AM

That is where my mind fails from simple exhaustion. 9:12 PM

> Yes. 8:42 AM

From the sheer effort of trying to process this. 9:12 PM

> Sometimes you must rest. 8:42 AM
>
> Sometimes your mind needs to think of other things. 8:42 AM
>
> Your spirit needs to imagine a different reality. 8:43 AM

I'll tell you what my secret refuge is ... 9:13 PM

And I don't know how you'll judge it. 9:13 PM

> I won't – 8:44 AM

It's online shoe shopping. 9:14 PM

Well, that means you and my son Aijaz
have a lot in common. 8:44 AM

That is, when the internet is on. Which
it isn't, most of the time. 9:14 PM

Ha ha, Aijaz likes shoes?! 9:15 PM

And that means that if we come and are stuck under
curfew, I can promise him that consolation. 8:45 AM

Don't promise. 9:16 PM

He is OBSESSED with shoes. 8:46 AM

No, of course not. 8:46 AM

The curfew encompasses everything. 9:16 PM

The internet is a luxury. 9:16 PM

As is delivery ... 9:16 PM

Sigh, yes, delivery. 8:46 AM

We are back to being the country without a post office. 9:16 PM

Yes, I was just about to invoke Shahid's ghost. 8:47 AM

☺ 9:17 PM

As we were texting, Aijaz was getting
ready for school. 8:48 AM

I had bought him a pair of purple
sneakers in the summer ... 8:48 AM

And he had left them at his grandmother's house. 8:48 AM

And he had called her and asked her to
bring them this morning. 8:49 AM

She was on her way to the gym. 8:49 AM

And I was reading the part about your niece's experience
of vanquishing the soldiers in her Eid finery. 8:50 AM

And I couldn't help sobbing when I read that ... 8:50 AM

And I told him what had happened. 8:50 AM

His grandmother came, and he put on the shoes and gave me a comforting hug. 8:51 AM

All I have is this WhatsApp heart. 🖤 9:24 PM

I wish us all healing. 9:25 PM

And more purple sneakers. 9:25 PM

Ameen. 9:25 PM

I wish you purple sneakers (or high-heeled Jimmy Choos) of Azaadi! 8:58 AM

Ameen! 9:28 PM

Please give Aijaz a hug of solidarity from me. 9:28 PM

Bilkul. Aijaz uses his internet time to look at soccer shoes / sneakers and will be delighted that you do too. 8:59 AM

✊ 9:30 PM

✌ 9:01 AM

2016-09-23

I just saw your FB status: "The earth loses its spin" – it says you posted it sixteen hours ago. Last night at about 8:30 p.m., Aijaz read to me from a nerdy science book called *What If?* 3:08 PM

He says it is his most favourite book. *Serious Scientific Answers to Absurd Hypothetical Questions.* And last night he insisted on reading the entire first section. It's an answer to the question, "What would happen if the earth and all terrestrial objects suddenly stopped spinning, but the atmosphere retained its velocity?" It then devotes about five pages to detailing the various apocalyptic outcomes. And then it talks about the moon! 3:09 PM

Sending love and solidarity. 3:16 PM

2016-09-24

Wow! 8:18 PM

2016-10-04

Sumayya, I ordered this book, *Of Gardens and Graves*, in August and it finally arrived on Friday.[1]

It feels like such a relief to start reading it. Thoughtful sentences and paragraphs and pages, not angry reactive tweets and illegible hashtags. Also, the poems appear in transliterated (in Roman letters) Koshur, as well as the English translations. So I can do something about my non-existent ability in that language, at least. 8:03 AM

That sounds so therapeutic. 8:37 PM

It is, exactly. 8:07 AM

Just the fact that a literary scholar who happens to be a Pandit gathered all these poems from Kashmiris who only write in Kashir and worked diligently to translate them is healing. Bringing people together on the page. 8:08 AM

Tell me how you are. 8:11 AM

Honestly, I don't know anymore. I guess I am going through a phase of growth. And reinforcement. But it feels like a performance. In front of an audience of shadows. 8:42 PM

What is being reinforced? 8:15 AM

I am spending my time being pulled between several different pieces of writing. 8:18 AM

All of them somehow demanding a share of my time simultaneously. 8:18 AM

And what I am forced to keep thinking about is the way men behave towards women. Men of my "community." 8:20 AM

I was raised here in Canada with this very
strong sense of being "Muslim" ... 8:20 AM

and part of the work I am doing is to uncover and
retrace the steps of the toll that has taken. 8:21 AM

A personal journey contained within the
journey of a community? 8:52 PM

On the community as a whole ... but I have to contend
every day with the toll it took on me. 8:22 AM

And it's hard to find the stamina to keep at the
writing and block everything out. 8:24 AM

I completely get this exhaustion. 8:54 PM

It is so difficult to surmount it. 8:54 PM

Yet surmounting it is essential to survival. 8:55 PM

Yes. Exactly. When you said, "in front of an audience of
shadows," I got that sense – of similar exhaustion. 8:25 AM

If the people around us cannot nourish
and sustain us, some part of ourselves has
to withdraw somewhere. 8:26 AM

And my most consistent source of sustenance
when I am alone is in books. 8:27 AM

Yes, the need to create a space that may be home,
even if it's within ourselves. 8:57 PM

Yes. 8:27 AM

Within and of ourselves we have to be respectful,
loving, gentle, appreciative. 8:28 AM

True. 8:59 PM

Yet we often get some of the harshest
treatment from within ourselves.

[untitled poem]

This morning,
Sickness
Spins the earth's gravitational field
A slight tilt
Of the axis
Hurtles the undigested debris of hunger
Through time and space

A sickness of movement
A churning numbness

How many days has it been
Since your last period?
Your last ice age

How long has it been since
A man fucked you   *carnal language*
Guarded virgin
Daughter of the tomb
Untouched by angels

This morning,
Sickness
Radiates
From a seed at the epicentre
Of your pleasureless tremors
A date seed
A stone
A pit

(How many centuries has it been
Since Yazid flirted
With penile innuendo
Over Karbala's arid soil)

This morning
Sickness
Consumes you from the heart outwards
Until stillborn words
Foam at the mouth of a black hole

Go scream labour in the beautiful mid-October desert
of a curfewed Kashmir
Hold on to the trunk of a date palm
Give birth
To the earth that you're pregnant with

Rozabal's distraught Jesus

His first cry a Word
... when the Word was with God,
... when the Word was, "God!"

8:59 PM

2016-10-13

This is a very powerful piece ... 10:47 AM

a controlled rage that smoulders white
hot for seven stanzas. 10:51 AM

The crucial words we need are yours ... 10:53 AM

not Jesus's and not God's. 10:53 AM

Thank you for the ricochet, dear Rahat. 11:43 PM

I keep reading it over and over. 1:00 PM

The way it builds – every line is necessary. 1:01 PM

"Your last period? / your last ice age" – so
jarring and perfect & 1:06 PM

"From a seed at the epicentre
Of your pleasureless tremors"

– an earthquake I didn't know I was waiting for. 1:06 PM

Your linked metaphors of earth as
woman's body – 1:07 PM

2016-10-14

Rahat, I am so honoured by your
attention to these lines. 1:38 AM

2016-10-13

Your vision is razor-sharp here. You bear witness to the turbulence and upheaval arising from the earth's tilted axis, the woman's body in struggle. Balance can be restored only by speaking the body's truth against the Yazids of this earth. Speaking the truth of her body is more powerful than all tyrannical attempts to subjugate her. It is nothing less than the truth of the earth. 1:23 PM

2016-10-14

Rahat, I am utterly honoured as well as warmed by your reading of it. 1:57 AM

2016-10-13

Please write more. Jesus may be bewildered that curfew could rule over such a beautiful October in Kashmir, but the woman, the poet, possesses full knowledge of how curfew constrains her body. She is the one to survive it. 1:34 PM

2016-10-23

Give this a listen:

Link to a YouTube video of "Ishmael," musical Quran recitation by South African jazz composer and musician Abdullah Ibrahim. 12:07 PM

Jazz = zikr. 12:07 PM *devotion*

2016-11-01

I have been carrying this handbag you sent me from Srinagar everywhere. It is the perfect size for everything I need to take with me. I got caught in the rain, so it has been drying off in front of the fire. 5:11 PM

2016-11-02

This makes me very happy! 7:28 AM

I have almost never bought my own handbags –
Kashmiri women somehow always manage to provide
me with a steady supply. 7:55 AM *this is cute*

2016-11-13

Salam. How are you? Does the country have a post
office? Are any letters or packages reaching you? 1:03 PM

2016-11-14

Rahat – I am alright, as much in control of myself as I *prayer of invocation*
seem capable of. No – nothing reaches here, not even du'ā *or*
it seems. How are you coping with the despair? 8:02 PM *help from God*

With the determination to go down fighting.
Under the reasoning that I am still free to walk
the streets and breathe the cold air. 4:30 PM

It's funny – I somehow feel as if you have been with me
when I have given all these readings at different venues,
and that this must all be familiar to you. 8:37 PM

2016-11-16

You would have loved anyone who walked with
you along such streets to such an end. 3:09 PM

!! 3:09 PM

Dear God ... 3:09 PM

For some reason I haven't been able to stop thinking
of Aijaz the past couple of days. 3:12 PM

Imagine him playing cricket with my nephew
in my mother's garden! 3:13 PM

It's just an image pinned to my brain. 3:13 PM

Thank you for the غزل. 3:15 PM

I imagine you reading it to a bunch of young
Kashmiri poets at Goodfellas. 3:16 PM

Love that image – will likewise pin it to mine. 7:15 PM

2016-12-11

The snow fell on Musqueam Land over a few days
last week. I went out walking among the heavily
blanketed trees and felt the almost ridiculous return
of a kind of peace. Environmentally induced smiling.
Highly irregular facial expression. 4:53 PM

2016-12-12

I learned to appreciate the joy of walking from you – of feet
touching the earth and the surface of the earth buoying you
back – affording you an unmediated rhythm of connection
that is yet to be monetized. Your feet on Musqueam Land
and Musqueam snow connect you to old-town Srinagar that
awaits this year's first snowfall, but the lanes afford me a
rare freedom stolen from the curfew – a freedom that only
being on foot can provide. Transported within vestibules
of metal and plastic and gasoline, we evade freedom as well
as continuity with the earth that helps us stay grounded in
lands where we belong and lands that belong to us. 6:03 PM

I wish you more peace and more smiling and more
organic links with your environment. 6:04 PM

2016-12-13

Dear Sumayya, I am going to exercise the demons of
2016 with a poetry reading on my birthday, inshallah.
It will be a small gathering of women writers. I
would like to read your poem and talk about our
ongoing curfewed exchange. Ijazat hai? 8:15 AM

Of course! Would you like me to share
an updated version? 9:49 PM

> Yes, by all means. 8:35 AM

2016-12-25

> Christmas Mubarak, Sumayya jan. I hope
> you & family are well. 9:19 AM

2016-12-26

Christmas Mubarak to you too, dear Rahat. I
hope you have a beautiful time. 11:09 AM

2017-01-02

Sending you thoughts of love and respect. 7:54 PM

Also sharing a poem from a while ago:

> [untitled poem]
>
> There's a world and a half between us
> There's a hush and a storm between us
> There are a flock of birds
> And a swarm of bees between us
>
> Shakespeare's ghost, unbearable offspring, half of a love story
> Three murders and sixteen broken hearts
> There's Facebook, there's Gmail, there's a search history
> Between us
>
> There's that echo of an echo
> Some lilac, some lavender, some citrus between us
> There's a playlist between us
>
> There is a constant falling
> And a sporadic pulse
> Between us
> There are stones, and dust, and discourse
> And a line of actual control between us
>
> There is her, and there is him
> There are so many of them between us

There are years between us
There are noises between us
There is a universe of meaning between us

There's a tropical rainforest, there's an old Delhi restaurant,
There's a beautiful masjid between us
There are refugees, occupations, catastrophes between us

There is God

Between you and me

Is a body of salt water
A quaint little bonfire
Stolen land
And borrowed breath.

8:02 PM

> Thank you so much.
>
> "There are a flock of birds / And a swarm of
> bees between us" – perfect. 11:26 AM

2017-01-12

May you have a beautiful birthday, Rahat.
And beautiful times ahead. 12:50 PM

> Thank you, dear Sumayya. 😊 And may I enjoy
> some of those times in your company. 8:25 AM

Inshallah, that is a pleasure I will always
look forward to. 11:35 PM

Also, since I consider you my پیر on modern
urban spaces, this reminds me strongly of you,
and I imagine you reading it out: 😄 😄

> Link to a cartoon by Tom Gauld, "The Life-Changing Magic of Decluttering
> in a Post-Apocalyptic World." 11:45 PM

> ✊ 😊 You know, even naskh with "Abrogation"
> you has elegance. 10:23 PM

[Handwritten annotations:]

Abrogation is the repeal or abolition of a law, right, or agreement

Naskh is also a smaller, round script of Islamic calligraphy

"Abrogation" it recognizes that one rule might not always be suitable for every situation

27

2017-02-05

> It's snowing again in Vancouver ... thick piles
> of white winter slush everywhere. 4:32 PM

2017-02-06

I have noticed from my FB feed that Vancouver
and Srinagar have been experiencing snow
more or less in sync this winter. 9:16 PM

2017-02-06

And it's the same slush here now. 9:17 PM

2017-02-06

The many states of water. 9:56 PM

2017-02-24

> How are you doing? Are you still going to marry
> the fellow you mentioned last fall? I really love
> the photos you have been posting – 1:43 PM

2017-02-25

Thank you Rahat ... I am well, alhamdulillāh. No, I called it
off with him a few days before the wedding. How have you
been? Oh, I finally received *Cosmophilia*! Thank you. 8:53 AM

2017-02-26

> Did you receive the copy I mailed
> you from Delhi??? 7:38 PM

> I want a photo of you with my book in
> Srinagar please please!! 7:39 PM

2017-02-27

Yes, that copy. 🖤 🖤 10:38 PM

And soon I'll take that picture, inshallah. 10:38 PM

| It has just started snowing again. 10:09 AM

2017-03-11

There was a little sunny patch this afternoon, a perfect moment of cosmophilia, so I took out the book, walked to the dargah[2] and sat by the lake for a bit, going through some of the poems.

A shrine or tomb built over the grave of a revered Sufi saint or dervish

Photo of Rahat Kurd's book *Cosmophilia* against a backdrop of Dal Lake and snowy mountains under a cloudy sky and a few overhanging willow fronds. 3:22 PM

| This is wonderful. As if I can feel the cold air
| and the endurance of the mountains. 1:38 PM

2017-03-12

Thank you, Rahat, for the beauty and strength in your words.

[untitled poem]

The city one keeps waking up from as nightmare
Must always have coffee shops –
Gentrified and gentrifying –
Selling the same dream
In varying concentrations of caffeine

One walks such a city
Barefoot
The touch of its spun-sugar bee-stung soil
A strange ritual of grounding
To several versions of reality

A wet dream made unerotic
Through interpretation

Its insistence on life as insomnia
Is matched only by its listless obsession
With driving, being driven, and the drive to rush past everything,
To neither touch nor be touched

To neither be nor not be

So in April we meet at a café
On the corner of Granville and Khayam
(One is tempted to spell it Khayyām,
Except there is neither jug of wine
Nor book of verse
Neither wilderness nor paradise
Underneath the bough)
Over a hurried conversation
As if the wind were rushing after us,
And the clouds were flying after us,
And the moon were plunging after us,
And the whole wild night were in pursuit of us,
But so far, we were pursued by nothing else

So one sleepwalks
From city to city
A refugee from rain

The Tropic of Poetry, dear Rahat,
Stretches from Vancouver to Srinagar,
From April to September

A dull arc of blasphemy
A shower of stones
In the best of times
In the worst of times

10:41 AM

2017-05-13

"So one sleepwalks

From city to city

A refugee from rain

The Tropic of Poetry, dear Rahat,

Stretches from Vancouver to Srinagar,

From April to September

A dull arc of blasphemy

A shower of stones

In the best of times

In the worst of times" 10:15 PM

2017-05-14

It's amazing, Rahat, I'm rereading "April Is When I Most
Hate Vancouver"[3] right at this moment! 10:46 AM

2017-05-13

Dear Sumayya: Having said these lines of yours over to
myself many times, I am working on a reply! 10:17 PM

2017-05-14

We're in perfect sync. 10:47 AM

I await your reply. 10:48 PM

2017-05-13

I want to talk to someone in publishing about
this poetic exchange we're having. You know,
no one ever asks me a thing about Kashmir. I
mean in connection to my work. 10:19 PM

2017-05-14

That is odd, given how much Kashmir is
present in your work. 10:50 AM

And you seem present in Kashmir. 10:50 AM

2017-05-13

It's beyond odd – it compounds my alienation. 10:20 PM

I was walking and thinking about you under
curfew and writing the new draft yesterday. I
will type it up tonight. Do you know Shahid's
poem "A Dream of Glass Bangles"? 10:25 PM

A widow smashing the rivers on her arms! 10:56 AM

2017-05-13

> Yes!! 10:27 PM
>
> It is one of his early poems and arguably slight, compared to the poems in *Country* and *Rooms* – but it came back to me, and then I found something I wrote in an older notebook ... 10:29 PM

2017-05-14

Would you share that? 11:00 AM

2017-05-13

> A quick fragment:

[untitled poem]

Where am I loosed to wander
these August evenings?
If nothing must keep me indoors tonight; if nothing must let me go.
The feeling returns of the mountains etched on night sky in Kashmir,
moths at dusk hovering under cottage light,
your surprise at the continual rush
of the river after dark,
and the way, writing this, I am still there,
in the bend of time at the tip of my pen –
stop to listen, hear the river white with melted glacier's foam,
hear your sighing aunts,
their silks releasing perfumed heat after the banquet's crush,
their voices a music of affection – calling across the dark – did she break
    her bangles? – ah, take care, watch for stones, take care of those
    lovely glass bangles!

10:44 PM

2017-05-14

Wow. You bring the rivers and the bangles together
in a way that Shahid couldn't. 11:23 AM

😄 11:24 AM

🙂At that point I had not read the Shahid poem for a long time. But the memory is based on my childhood and teen summers in Kashmir! I don't know if I was also remembering his poem unconsciously ... 10:56 PM

You want to usher Kashmir into your here **Writing the Now** and now, which is your poetry. 11:27 AM

And people only want to read those as fragments of a past. A "Kashmiri background." It isn't a background for you. It's where parts of you are actively playing out. 11:28 AM

Yes. I have been thinking about rebellion. How my writing has to be that. 10:59 PM

To push at the complacencies of this grey concrete know-nothing city. 11:00 PM

Grey concrete know-nothing city. 😄😄😄 11:32 AM

I need to sleep. I will send you the poem draft soon. 11:18 PM

Shab ba kheyr, Rahat. 11:49 AM

Shab ba kheyr until soon. 2:26 AM

Salam Sumayya. Do you remember an early morning sky photo you took, of some birds on the roof of your house in Srinagar? Do you remember when you took that image & posted on FB? 4:32 PM

I do! I was visiting my parents in 2011 or 2013, I think. 9:21 AM

> It must have been the fall of 2013. October, possibly? I was working on some new poems for *Cosmophilia* at the time, but I wrote several lines in pencil in the same notebook, in an undated entry, about that photo. 8:17 AM

I took the picture on Sept. 4, 2013. Must have shared it on FB around that time. 8:40 AM

This blue-green, full-of-secrets city looks terrifyingly beautiful this morning. Sending you love. 8:41 AM

> Thank you! These are wonderful – and that is the pink sky I remember. 7:53 AM

2017-05-29

We are under internet curfew once again. 12:15 PM

> I heard the news earlier today. Another extrajudicial killing. 4:19 AM

2017-06-01

Fragments 1

> *On my mother's arms*
> *were bangles like waves of frozen rivers*
> —Agha Shahid Ali, "A Dream of Glass Bangles"

Where am I loosed to wander
these August evenings?
If nothing must keep me inside tonight
If nothing must let me go

Beyond the mountains
refracting this city's glare
my memory retrieves an image
of mountains etched on a Kashmir night
moths hovering under cottage-light,
the surprising rush, continual,
of the river after dark,
and the way, writing this,
I am still there,
in the bend of time at the tip of my pen.

I hear the river
white with melted glacier foam
I hear the aunts sighing,
remember silk releasing perfume
after the banquet's crush

Their calling voices
a music of affection
across the grassy banks

Are you wearing those glass bangles?
Take care, watch out for stones,
take care of those lovely glass bangles!

*

Fragments 2

From her curfewed morning
Sumayya sends me the sky above Srinagar,
lit by whatever dawn
the Himalayas permitted to pass.

A row of birds arrayed
as if ordered for the delight of everyone,
on the roof of her father's house.

I shut my eyes on Vancouver
and I shelter under it,
that sky she sent for my safekeeping
the same one I unfurled there at fifteen
lying on my back amid the rocks at Aharbal
when I knew my happiness was about to end

Stretching out my arms,
silently commanding the cosmos
to keep the sky safely pinned
above Kashmir in my absence
absorbing all I could of its warmth

Though I could not have known
how long I'd need to make it last –
what penurious rate at which
I would have to draw it out,
over how many winters –
how false the economy
to which I would succumb.

Fragments 3

And this poem, tonight,
because of what weather does
to consciousness –
or is it the other way around
and is the origin even the point?

Drenched earth, pink tulips,
fading magnolias, honeysuckle
at the top of its game,
late cherry in tight clusters,
everything lightly speckled
in spite of the gloaming,
tips of leaves just visible
pushing from folded buds

If only there could have been a conversation tonight,
a weaving of memory a warm hand on the shoulder
blood pulsing inside skin
to carry your young summers forward
into your untold winters –
not this cascade of stalled, squandered years.

The truth has become distinct from lies
exactly the way it says in Surat al Baqarah

That this was always the wrong city,
the wrong year, the cold ache beneath the ribs
always marked the site of a strangeness
that shouldn't have hardened
into the shape of your life –

A strangeness you might have fled.
Why could your footsteps never ring
through streets where their approach
was eagerly awaited? Where is that city
the living lines of whose dead poets
you might have carried forward
from their late winters
into your untold summers?

Curfew pays out, in slow hours
counted by restless children
the erosions and erasures of Srinagar

A woman at Yaletown–Roundhouse Station
shakes rainwater off an iridescent umbrella
Now pink at one slant; now blue at another

I chafe against Vancouver's
brief prettiness in sun showers

What has this city done
to the shape of my Fridays?

Meaning detaches itself from calls to prayer
and minarets appreciate by the square foot
way out of my price range.

Clouds mimic the blank faces
of the men warily guarding the mosque
against the hearts of women
those superior houses of God

No measure weighs our sacred against their profane
No moral arc bends this weird coastal light

I scan the city for signs of rebellion,
signs to echo my will to leave forever

but commerce remains their only prescription
repellent substitute for belonging

I want to unlearn this appetite
seek another satiety –
Continuity. Ongoingness.
The means to live with myself.

If, from Cordoba to Fez,
from Bombay to Melaka,
from Aleppo to Kashgar
any woman walking alone
cannot retrace the corridors
of her ancient multiplicities

If we have subsisted on crumbs of memory
in the silence following their destruction –
could our acts of inscription
be our true acts of rebellion?

To write upon the surfaces of our exclusion
until we carve a doorway into belonging.

8:28 AM

2017-06-01

Thank you for sharing "Fragments" with me, a gestalt of
the Kashmir we both inhabit, in two distinct spaces and
times. It helps me make the cracks bearable. 9:45 PM

2017-06-27

It's Eid. Send news when you can.
Sending love as always. 7:56 AM

Hi Rahat, Eid mubarak! I do not have much news apart
from what is already documented, relayed, and properly
mourned in voices we still retain. The only thing I can add to
them is a translucent layer of personal insanity, my extreme
disgust with Kashmiri patriarchy, and the bravado of my
own belief in (desperation after) redemption. 6:03 PM

Here's a lone street ride that I saw on my way back
home from my Nani's yesterday: 6:04 PM

I didn't think they had these anymore. 6:04 PM

We used to have them in my grandfather's backyard (The
Martyrs' Graveyard) on Eids when I was a child. 6:05 PM

It seemed extra desolate on this Eid. I hitched my
niece on to it. She was confused. 6:05 PM

And here are all the girls in their glittery best. And the
guys already trying to flirt via Bollywood tunes. 6:07 PM

A priceless photo essay infused with your inimitable wryness, o tour guide. 9:30 AM

That tiny little Ferris wheel. God! 10:00 AM

2017-07-03

After Eid + Pride in Toronto, I went to my mother's house in Ottawa last week. Just a few days spent among the women of my family. Aijaz is spending this summer performing in a youth production of *Romeo and Juliet*. He began full-time rehearsals with his cast and directors today. The soccer player has opted to immerse himself in the language of Shakespeare. 12:16 PM

2017-07-05

Société canadienne des postes

A spider's nest at the heart
of a grief the size of Kashmir:
This is the story of a story
That left nothing to imagination
Except leaves

The shape
And texture
Of cobwebs

In chapter twenty-nine, "The Most Tenacious of Homes"
The heart is a wily predator
Weaving a rope of silk
Into an elaborate noose
Spanning decades

The plot thickens
In "The Early Aughts"
A flurry of flights and fireflies
Dreams dissolve into dreams
Until nothing remains of reality
But a lace curtain
Sheer as cobwebs

Love's air-bending surrogate
Male Protagonist-in-Chief
Braids words
To each page of "The Heavenly Ascension"
Zipping past memory
At the speed of sound

A spider's heart in a nest of leaves
An archive of longing
From East to West

A chest of journals
The size of a coffin
Has arrived by mail

9:50 AM

2017-07-05

You make some very striking image
juxtapositions. 6:48 PM

2017-07-07

It has been one year since they killed Burhan Wani
and my return to Kashmir began to unravel. 11:20 PM

Kashmiri militant leader killed by Indian Army

"The heart is a wily predator
Weaving a rope of silk
Into an elaborate noose
Spanning decades"

Rereading this today. These lines especially. And the absorbing relay between spider, web, and subtle play on "leaves" – and the sudden jump to the image of "coffin" as burial site of written memory. 6:32 PM

PART TWO

The Machine Has My Eyes and It Uses Them to Un-See

Salam Rahat. I have been performing "productivity"
for the University-Industrial Complex. If I had any
affinity left for academia, working a clerical job in a
Third-World university has wiped me clear of that.

MOOD

The last three years of global warming in Kashmir have
turned the summer terribly humid. But I have managed to
trek up Zabarwan on the weekends. It is the only respite.

My parents' house is being renovated for my brother's
wedding next year.

My grandmother's days here may be numbered. I kissed her
on her forehead last Friday, and she clasped my hand and
wouldn't let go. She said I always give her the best foot rubs.

My little cousin was just hit by the Indian army with
a pellet gun; his chest is riddled with tiny holes.
He has the cutest dimples when he smiles.

I read nothing and write nothing. 10:55 PM

The coastal Vancouver sunlight today is completely
obscured by smoke from out-of-control forest fires in
the interior. One ought to pray for rain, but I want the
sun to shine on my son's nightly outdoor Shakespeare
performances, whose magic keeps me going. In the
past month, the pressure to perform productivity
has been heavy on my head. I have been applying for
jobs between writing deadlines, to bind my fate more
deeply to this hard-hearted city. (Aijaz is starting
high school this September and is outgrowing shoes
at a rapid pace.) If I am not hired – or even if I am – I
would like to bring you your glass bangles. 2:34 PM

2017-08-06

Dear Rahat, may God expand your resources and your rizq, so that Aijaz has a steady supply of shoes whenever he wants them. May the magic of the moon shine on his performances, and may the haze clear from our lives. I have come to hate Vancouver without any reservations / qualifications.

Would you consider moving to Kashmir at some point?

I went to Sonmarg with family yesterday, cherishing whatever days I am blessed with to spend with them. I am resisting tremendous pressure to get married. I could trust you with my glass bangles, whenever the universe conspires to bring us to the same city. 11:57 PM

Those bangles have been on my mind ever since we talked about the waves of frozen rivers. 11:57 AM

They were my father's wedding gift to me, since I requested to not have any gold. 11:58 AM

He said he wouldn't know how to shop for bangles, since the fragile weight of performative masculinity and its attendant incompetencies was on his shoulders. 11:58 AM

But I insisted. 11:59 AM

And he bought me six of the most beautiful sets of glass bangles ever. 11:59 AM

Turquoise, baby pink, mustard, black, ivory, purple. 11:59 AM

A few of them broke when I brought them to Kuala Lumpur from Srinagar after marriage. 12:00 PM

A few more broke when I brought them to Vancouver from KL. 12:00 PM

I cannot bear the thought of any more breaking in transit from Vancouver to Srinagar. 12:01 PM

I have been requesting F. to send me my stuff, my books and childhood journals and a few cherished baubles. 12:02 PM

I never asked for the bangles, though. 12:02 PM

I hope they're safe wherever he has put them. 12:02 PM

Thank you for sending me the sukoon of your words and the marvellous green valley. Reading your message as I sat down to eat a peach (in the very Prufrockian manner) with bites of pastry and sips of coffee feels as though I am eating breakfast in your company. 12:13 PM

I had woken up today with the question hanging over me – tomorrow is Monday; will they call me tomorrow? "They" being the NGO to which I sent my résumé over a week ago. I keep thinking of the job as a potential anchor for me – to financial independence in this city while Aijaz is in high school – but before I happened to come across the job listing, my heart was full of thoughts of fleeing from here; of wondering whether I could make provision for him elsewhere. Cities I have walked around, met writers in, seen artists perform in, and feel I would be content to live in: Montréal, Manhattan, Brooklyn, Toronto. I also thought – what if I brought Aijaz home to Srinagar? I want intensely to break him out of the Vancouver bubble, for him to have the feeling of home elsewhere and in at least one other language he could actually use, rather than me struggling to pass it on to him, at such a far remove. 12:17 PM

If I get the job, I will be in a position to plot and plan carefully. 12:21 PM

Did I ever tell you that my father (who had a Kurdish-speaking ironsmith father, whom I never met, because he died when my father was still a boy) worked in a glass factory when he moved to Canada? He and his older brother were hired in Hamilton, a few days after they left Karachi and landed in Toronto. 1

Hamilton was known for its steel factories when I was growing up. Glass and metal a substances I dream upon. 12:29 PM

And, of course, cement – the substance my mother's father worked with, to make tiles and planters, a few of which I still possess. Last year, on the night of July 8, we had a Critical Muslims Eid dinner here in the coastal city. July 8 is my mother's birthday. I had posted a photo of her hugging Aijaz at the Toronto airport (from a few months before, in April) to her FB page to wish her a happy birthday. In one more week, on July 15, Aijaz and I were scheduled to fly to meet her, my aunt, my sister, and my cousin at the Toronto airport; from there we were all going to fly to Delhi and then Srinagar. You remember. 12:36 PM

Anyway, that Friday night, the eighth, at East Is East on Main Street, where I had gathered with the Muslims, F. joined our group with a friend who told us he was from Shiraz, another city I dream of returning to, impossible as it seems. I met several new people that evening – and yet there was a feeling of Eid al Fitr, a true sense of celebration, among us. I happily told everyone where I would shortly be taking my son. And F. asked if I would take some things of yours along, and I said I would be glad to. And we agreed he would drive over with them a few days before the fifteenth. And the next morning I woke up to the news of the killings and the curfew. 12:48 PM

By the time F. messaged me to ask for a drop-off time, my mother and aunt had decided to cancel our flights. 12:50 PM

Tell me, has F. been able to send you any of your other belongings? Do you know if he still has the bangles? Earlier in the winter of 2016, when I went to Delhi, he had asked me to bring your laptop. And then I keep remembering how it took a year for my book to get to you in Srinagar from Delhi. It makes me dizzy and chronology loses meaning. 1:38 PM

I don't know what to offer you as resistance against the pressure to get married. Only the evidence of your own self. Your strength. 4:07 PM

After I got married, I remembered for a very long time the audible and visible relief on the faces of so many people who thought my engagement meant that now they knew something about me. 4:08 PM

Also, that I became an object of chatter by people on the periphery of my life. 4:09 PM

Because I had entered that familiar, safe category of feminine being. 4:12 PM

I think the patriarchy that pressures women to value marriage as some kind of indicator of our social worth also produces the privilege that allows men to lie, cheat, and deny women's rights. Men are sheltered from accountability while women are pressured to conform to society's hypocritical standards. 4:31 PM

This deeper social structure pre-emptively supports freedom and ease for men unconditionally. This entrenched system of patriarchy looks and feels, at the moment when you plan the wedding, like the loving pressure of a family, friends, and community who want a reason to celebrate you. 4:35 PM

2017-08-07

Yes … We are literally sold into marriages in exchange for what we're told is our parents' happiness. It is especially easy to succumb to this when you're already ridden with guilt about having caused them much pain. 10:40 AM

It is impossible to exist as a woman for your own sake. 10:41 AM

it's a continues cycle bc her parents were likely told the same thing — to think about their parents happiness.

That's it. We must exist for our own sake – it is so generative to claim this right. It's not selfish at all: It really is only possible to give to others in the abundance that comes from holding on to your own fearless self.

I want you to hold on to the right to demand your parents' love and support while you resist that pressure. To insist on living in serenity and peace, regardless of social outrage denied its slice of wedding cake, is a radical act. Marriage, in principle, is very fine. But being pressured and guilted into it against one's will never is. 11:35 PM

And it never can be. A marriage made under pressure must crack. 11:37 PM

Thank you for sending me strength, Rahat. 1:14 PM

Thank you for being there for me. Thank you for keeping Kashmir alive in my heart and mind. 12:42 PM

2017-08-23

I am reading Arundhati Roy's new novel. It is as if she has stuffed her head full of Kashmir and put it all between the covers of a book. I have never read anything with such amazement alternating with resentment. It would have been better if I could have read it during the smoke-haze days, because then I would feel as if I were listening to a storyteller in Delhi, and I could feel uncomplicatedly grateful for her gifts. The sky is clear now and after every few pages I have to sneeze.

I didn't get the job. Or even interviewed. Instead, the hiring person called me to explain their decision and sent me a list of ten other job openings in what she called "the sector," assuring me that my qualifications were excellent. It was a rare moment of unexpected civility in this brittle season.

Earlier this month, in Delhi, Reyhan Chaudhuri's father and mother died, within a few days of each other. It's an incalculable loss, dear Sumayya. Their marriage – a Muslim and a Hindu – and the story of how they came together and the world they created together – itself constitutes a kind of rich alternative history of Delhi. When I visited in 2016, Reyhan's father gave me a pinstriped grey wool Nehru vest which suits me quite well, even if it's too large. Reyhan's mother had begun to lose her short-term memory, but she enjoyed my telling her that I had been to her house thirty years earlier when she had got a birthday cake for Rabia, my little sister, who turned five during our visit. At her dining table on the day I was invited to lunch, she kept asking why I had not brought my son, and repeatedly urged me to bring him next time. I feel this additional layer of loss, that Aijaz will never meet them, keenly. 10:18 PM

2017-09-01

Dear Sumayya, Eid Mubarak from me, Aijaz, my mother, and my sister in Ottawa. May we meet again in Srinagar. May peace be upon us all. 7:53 AM

Dear Rahat, Eid Mubarak. Forgive my tardiness in responding to you, although I love the "ongoingness" of this conversation.

It seems that as part of the universe's movement towards loss, you lost your dear aunt and uncle, and I lost my dear grandmother, whom I have known as the bravest, most eloquent, and wittiest of people. May they rest in God's infinite mercy.

This morning my boss at work gave me a "pep-talk" about how all my time belongs to "the institution." He literally said that my body, mind, and soul are paid for by the institution. I hope you're able to sort out your livelihood situation without having to sell yourself. As part of my resistance to the tyranny of capitalist productivity, I have been increasingly looking into the option of starting a small floriculture venture on a parcel of land just outside Srinagar. I mean, growing flowers for a living would be a nice way to fuck with oppression as well as Occupation. We need literally to own this land and to occupy it with our bodies and our trees and our rice and our flowers before we are occupied out of the land we belong to by our colonizers.

TBH

Also, I am planning to plant narcissi by my grandmother's grave. She loved nargis. She loved perfume and surma and Farsi poetry, a lot of which she had memorized by heart as a young girl, and which she would translate for us with disdain because she couldn't stand people who didn't understand Farsi.

she sounds cool ☺

In the last few days of her life, she was paralyzed by a major stroke and opening her terribly green eyes was her only way of responding to me.

Dear Rahat, please make du'ā for her. The happiest memories of my childhood are from her. Our most cherished stories, the family folklore, is passed down from her. They have been repeated to the point of mythology. Our wittiest inside jokes are from her.

I have read and reread your messages about the power and resilience and beauty in your line of womanhood and grandmotherhood. How their experiences of the world, and their sense perception, has shaped your own. How they, and the places they belong to, also belong to you.

I hope you have a lovely day. Please give my regards to your mum, and love to Aijaz. I send you the ecstasy of a beautiful early fall from Srinagar, the air is as limpid as my grandmother's eyes before they glazed over with cataracts. The internet will soon be snapped on Eid day, and we can't pray Eid namaz at Jamia Masjid because it is barricaded. 11:40 PM

Thank you so very much for this Sumayya jan – I absolutely loved reading about your grandmother as your source of culture and wit and her love of Farsi poetry and her impatience with requests for translation. I will think of her and make du'ā for her, and for the narcissi, and your ventures in floriculture. Inna lillahi, wa inna ilayhi rajioon, wa internet azadi zindabad. 4:54 PM

"Growing flowers for a living would be a nice way to fuck with oppression as well as Occupation." This phrase makes me very happy. 5:39 PM

Have I told you that I spent almost two months in Iran when I was still a newlywed? 6:09 PM

2017-09-02

You haven't. 7:14 AM

What you said about your grandmother's love of Farsi poetry reminded me. I was there in 1998. It was the first time I had ever been to a country where I didn't speak the language. And I couldn't read it or make sense of it from the street signs. I remember as we entered the first town we stayed in – Bam – I was appalled by my ignorance. 7:04 PM

Urdu and French had gotten me through many other places and situations and here they were no good at all. 7:05 PM

I thought, why did I not try to study it just a little before I came? The feeling of inadequacy never left me. 7:06 PM

And then, the first thing I did after I became truly single and alone again, in the spring of 2011, was to enroll in a modern Farsi evening class at a little TESL college not far from my apartment. It was an act of instinctive self-reclamation. I was determined to recover my multilingual fluencies. I was shocked at myself for not realizing how long I had been trapped in a monolingual existence. 7:35 PM

But my Persian ambitions have been repeatedly blocked. My first instructor had to go back to Tehran after four months; then in 2013 the college hired another instructor whom I studied with for a year, then the college itself packed up and moved to the International Village Mall, which was too far for me to follow. This year in the spring I met with a Farsi instructor at UBC and she assessed my reading level, but the class that I want to take won't be offered for another year. 7:40 PM

I read poems to try to keep Farsi in my life, in the meantime. I think I must send you some poems of Forugh Farrokhzad. I spent a chunk of money ordering her collection from a university press in the U.S. early this year. It's a bilingual edition. 7:43 PM

I have Farrokhzad's *A Rebirth* in my Amazon cart. And Amazon suspended services to Kashmir, so it'll make me very happy to receive one from you. 8:27 AM

Wonderful. 7:58 PM

Provided, of course, that any international couriers still deliver to Kashmir. 8:28 AM

I can photograph some of the poems and attach them here. 8:00 PM

(When I am back in Vancouver.) 8:01 PM

(In a few more days.) 8:01 PM

Though I know it isn't as satisfying to read as on paper ... poem photography *is* an expanding social-media genre. 8:03 PM

Ha ha, yes. 8:33 AM

Speaking of photography: I am just doing some finishing edits on my review essay of the new Arundhati Roy novel. And the editor asked me to think of an image to publish with it, and this morning in my jetlagged state (Aijaz & I flew back to Vancouver yesterday) I have just thought of your wonderful mirror-like image of Srinagar with the snowy mountain backdrop – the photo you captioned "City of my heart." Would you consider letting us publish it? The publication is called *Rungh.* I could send you my piece to read & you could decide? 5:50 AM

Of course, I'll be happy to have you use it. 6:24 PM

Please share your write-up with me if you can. 6:27 PM

I will. 6:27 AM

2017-09-16

Link to a YouTube voice recording of Iranian poet Forugh Farrokhzad reciting her poem "Tavalodi Digar" (another birth), first published in 1963. 8:45 AM

Reciting in her own voice. 8:45 AM

2017-09-22

Dear Sumayya, I see you are observing these days of remembrance of Muharram. Sending love and solidarity. I would love to know what the calligraphy in your profile says (I can only make out "Yawm Ashura"). How are you? I hope there are some roses blooming for you somewhere. 1:02 PM

> I am still revising my essay on Shahid and his mother. His evocation of her grief at Muharram is so powerful. He makes it all of Kashmir's. 1:04 PM

2017-09-23

Dear Rahat, Ashura coincides with a difficult phase in my mental health. I am obsessively attracted to vintage floral prints. Maybe it is just the wistful beauty / opulent wedding season of early autumn. But it is certainly my despair at being trapped in an inveterate language of loss. Rahat, I have no friends here. I speak to no one. This is an inside-out exile. 12:09 AM

My grandmother who just passed away was named Fatima. Ghulam Fatima. Shahid's mourning his mother stretches from Amherst to Karbala I first heard my grandmother say, "Kull ard Karbalā, w kull yawm 'Āshūrā': Every land is Karbala, every day is Ashura. The calligraphy in my profile picture. 12:09 AM

2017-09-22

> Thank you. 11:49 PM
>
> I can read it now. 11:49 PM
>
> I hate not being able to read beautiful scripts. 11:49 PM

2017-09-23

> Here is the published piece, finally:

Link to "Untouchable Kashmir," book review by Rahat Kurd published online at *Rungh* magazine. 6:08 PM

Salam Rahat, I saw you in a dream last night. We were at a protest in a town that seemed to be a strange combination of Vancouver and Srinagar. You got arrested. Your sunglasses were with me. 9:13 PM.

Wa salam dear Sumayya. I am trying to imagine the confrontational scenario where I turn to you to say, "Hold my sunglasses." 9:29 AM

It sounds eminently plausible. 9:31 AM

Yesterday afternoon, Kelty took me to VanDusen Botanical Garden. We walked amid ornamental tall grasses, deciduous trees, flowering bushes, heath, stands of bamboo and cedars. The leaves are turning in their slow deliberate way. 9:35 AM

Then we went into the gift shop. Kelty wanted some flower bulbs to plant at home. Kelty is a landscape architect – she once gave a talk at a fundraiser I organized, about the history and design of Shalimar, Nishat, and Naseem. I was astonished at her depth of knowledge – we had been friends for four years at that point, and still I hadn't known she had studied the Kashmiri Mughal gardens in school. The last time she came over to my place, I cooked saag and rice and I told her about your idea to grow flowers in an anti-colonial, anti-occupation enterprise, which she loved. 9:43 AM

Anyway, there were Kashmiri jamawar shawls for sale in the VanDusen Botanical Garden gift shop. 9:45 AM

A strange combination of Vancouver and Srinagar. 9:45 AM

Dear Rahat, last week I went on a date by the Jhelum near old Zero Bridge. The chinar park adjacent to the bridge (now turned into a restaurant / food court) has what would be a lovely walkway, perfect for a date away from the possibility of running into random members of the extended family. The loveliness of the context and meanings was in my head when the camera app on my phone happened to launch by chance and the one-eyed dajjal saw this very mundane and rather dispiriting scene:

In my mind I'm by the Jhelum, with the old Zero Bridge to my right; I am surrounded by chinars and the walk is full of the crunch of yellow leaves. But this is what it looks like to the camera. I thought of you. I told the guy about you and our exchanges. I don't know if I should have. I was overcome by something like wistfulness. 11:38 PM

2017-11-08

| Oh, that betrayer, the one-eyed dajjal. 1:04 PM

This was such an evocative report, Sumayya. Was the conversation with your date any good, at least? This week on Vancouver streets lined with massive old maples, there is a pinkish leaf powder flecked with yellow that sticks underfoot. I have been drained by the sameness of my quotidian routes in this city. When the days shorten (with the blessed relief of turning back the clock an hour), their repetitiveness becomes alternately soothing and numbing. I like the evenings, lighting the lamps, closing out the world, and equally I can be sickened by my inclination to burrow and hibernate. The sun in October was nearly blinding on some days – no softly smoky temperance, but the harshest, panicked climate-change glare. I steadied myself by taking photographs of the tree in my alley as it went from lush with brilliant red-orange to increasingly bare and austere over the seven days that marked the anniversary of my twentieth year in Vancouver. 10:15 PM

By November 3, the temperature dropped and the air stung my face. I had scolded Aijaz for leaving his coat at school on Monday. The one way I could defy the chill was to put on my own coat and go to the swimming pool. I have gone twice this week. I sit in the sauna with the grandmas and uncles of the Asian diasporas and we all are silent together and the heat pervades our bones and I remember what goodness feels like. 10:27 PM

Dear Sumayya, last night at the bookshop, with a small audience consisting entirely of my friends in the poetry community, I read four poems from *Cosmophilia*. I introduced them as "walking meditations" that were the result of my walks in Vancouver: "Burnaby, Evening, April," "Modern (Abdul Rehman)," "The Last Seven Minutes of *L'Eclisse*," and "Blue Glass Tulips."

The last one was especially satisfying, since I had never before read it in public and its subject matter suits the current (pre-Christmas) season. 5:11 PM

When I was deciding what to read for last night's event I felt as if I could now see how those four poems were connected in a way that escaped me when I was writing them. 5:15 PM

I took a screen cap of a poem you posted recently. I need to reread it a few times. I am working on some new ghazals and another long narrative poem called "Alkohol" (a substance I do not ingest but one which creates puzzles and obstacles for me nonetheless). 5:19 PM

I hope you are well and your family are all right. I have a few more things for you to read which I'll try to send you later this week. The sun set so early today and it was such a grey dark day and now I need to close my eyes. 5:23 PM

2017-11-30

I have wanted to read Cavafy for a long time and on Saturday I spotted this sunny little second-hand volume at Pulpfiction. So I bought it. I go only grudgingly into PF now because my favourite bookshop has become the Paper Hound. But I was hungry for noise and crowds and food, and also I wanted someone else's words to sit and look at for an hour. And then on the very first page was this direct admonition from beyond: 10:11 AM

The City

"I'll leave for other lands," you said, "I'll leave for other seas.
Another city better than this is certain to be found.
All my endeavours are by fate condemned;
and – like a corpse – my heart lies buried.
Till when will my mind go on wasting away.

Wherever I turn my gaze, wherever I look
I see my life gone to rack and ruin here,
where I spent and spoiled and squandered so many years."

You won't find new parts, won't find other seas.
The city will follow you. You'll wander its streets,
the same streets. And in the same districts you'll grow old;
and in these very same houses turn grey.
This is the city you'll always reach. Of places elsewhere
– don't hold out hope –
for you there's no boat, no path for you.
As you spoiled your life here
in this little corner, so you squandered it the world over.

> The text includes the original Greek. The translator's name is David Conolly. 10:12 AM

> I was dismayed when I read this. But maybe Cavafy doesn't belong to our conversation. Probably he is addressing someone totally outside the realm of our experiences. 10:20 AM

> A man, most likely. 10:21 AM

> I think the last two lines could only be addressed to a man. 10:22 AM

> The last two lines are where the poem turns foreboding and loses me. But maybe it has to be read politically and not personally. It's what a protester should say to a colonizer. 10:26 AM

> I'm also reading a book about Emily Dickinson.[4] The critic Helen Vendler writes detailed close reads of each poem. It is wonderful. I love and am surprised most of all by ED's cool detachment and religious skepticism. Nevertheless, if there does turn out to be a heaven, she has to be there. Or else I'm boycotting. 10:32 AM

2017-12-03

Rahat, I am going back to *Jane Eyre*, "There was no possibility of taking a walk that day." 9:07 PM

Sorry about lack of response from me. 9:08 PM

I am terribly, terribly cold and messages from you
are one of my sources of warmth. 9:08 PM

And I am sorry I am not able to reciprocate. 9:08 PM

Cosmophilia has been on my nightstand
the last two weeks or so. 9:09 PM

"Blue Glass Tulips." 9:10 PM

Spine up. 9:10 PM

2017-12-04

I can't read. 10:30 PM

> I think I am feeling some echo of the cold for you.
> Occupied Musqueam Land has been very wet and
> miserable, and the damp air chilled my bones
> yesterday. Kelty and I like a certain French pastry and
> chocolate shop called Thierry downtown. 10:39 AM

> But despite the dollars we have lavished on
> him, Thierry has not spent any on making
> a proper windproof patio. 10:39 AM

> And the shopper humans were taking up all the
> indoor tables. Kelty and I stood and gave the eye to
> a pair of young women who were sitting at a table
> with empty glasses who wouldn't leave. 10:41 AM

> But then we collected our dignity and went outside,
> and I became thoroughly chilled to the core. 10:42 AM

> Along with my coffee. 10:42 AM

> Are you able to travel? I think we should
> make plans to meet in 2018. 10:57 AM

> Just saw your FB post. May your loved one who passed away be enfolded in mercy. May you and your family be enfolded in love and mercy. Ameen. 12:14 PM

2017-12-14

Ameen! Thank you, Rahat. Thank you also for your thoughtful messages prior to this, those I haven't responded to yet, and for which I am sorry.

I should be able to travel in fall 2018, inshallah. Are you planning to visit Delhi? Jan. 2018 is also a good time for me to travel, although I realize it's at short notice for you. But I am hopeful we'll be able to see each other in the year of the puppy.

This winter there appears to be a long, drawn-out dry spell in Kashmir. That makes it extra dreary, and people are falling sick. But worst of all, my lovely niece and nephew have left to spend a few months with their mother's family in Malaysia, and their love has sustained me through the past few winters. We Skype daily. When I was in Vancouver, my niece was two, and she thought her puphi was trapped in Skype, and she has an elaborate mythology of how she managed to rescue me from it and bring me home. She has grown up enough to no longer think that Skype is an alternate dimension where loved ones are held captive, but she still thinks anyone using Skype on the regular is in need of help. 9:59 AM

101

How is your writing coming along? I sometimes see your reading engagements on Facebook. That is one of the things I miss most about Vancouver.

I have often wondered if Aijaz reads your work. Does he? Has he ever wanted to?

I just received my "Aadhaar" card, Modi's initiative to register the second-largest population on an electronic database, complete with iris patterns and fingerprints. The machine has my eyes and it uses them to un-see. I paid for this act of aggression with my own agency and took a day off work to give them my "biometrics," as they call them. I also regularly punch in at work using my biometrics. The inner clerk / archivist in me finds this satisfying, since information is neatly categorized and interlinked and hyperlinked. But the superficial poet in me is kinda dumbfounded at the metaphor lost somewhere in there. 10:11 AM

2017-12-15

No dystopic fiction I've read has been quite so cutting as your description of Modi Sarkar. "The machine has my eyes and it uses them to un-see." 9:09 AM

Aijaz is still too young to read my work. He has seen me read in public, but I'm quite thankful he isn't really interested in the content of my poems. Prototype Nuclear Rocket Ship. 9:54 AM

Sumayya, I typed the word "A-n-d" & realized that Aijaz has programmed it to automatically enter the words you see above. 9:55 AM

So even without the benefit of poetry, you see, he does enjoy wordplay. 9:56 AM

Malaysia sounds like an ideal place to spend a few months, although I have read that the winters are very rainy. 9:57 AM

It has been a grinding Prototype Nuclear Rocket Ship emotionally dry year here on occupied Coast Salish Lands. 10:00 AM

My plans of eventual escape help me keep going. 1:45 PM

(Deleted Aijaz's sneaky shortcut text.) 1:46 PM

2017-12-18

Dear Sumayya, I am facing the Days of Insurrection. Aijaz struggled to stay home from school today. He left and returned to the apartment; then he returned from the bus stop to the door and argued from the door panel to come back in; then he walked to the bus stop and called me to argue again; and I

remained steadfast and told him to keep walking
to the train if the bus wasn't coming. 10:40 AM

After all that, he got to school on time and
texted me: "This sucks." 10:41 AM

Three days until solstice and four more
days until the winter break. 10:41 AM

How are you? 10:42 AM

2017-12-19

Today is my mother's sixtieth birthday. I am struggling to
free her from the chokehold of YouTube videos and fake
news. She is going through an adolescence of her own.
She is alarmed by my anti-Saudi politics, but ever since
she heard a long-bearded guy go on a rant against Saudi
Arabia in English, she's convinced they're the devil.

My dad is obsessed with "health" apps.

It's just the three of us home for the winter, so my evenings
are desolate, given my parents' electronic addiction. 10:58 AM

I am stuck in a massive traffic jam on
the way to work. 10:59 AM

This highway is the worst thing about Srinagar. 10:59 AM

It is the lifeline of army supplies into the city. 11:00 AM

Oh God. Army of the damned. One of my lasting
memories from 1985 in Srinagar is of a vivid strip
of brown earth, like a gash in a hillside, which was
otherwise covered, naturally, and always had been, by
dense forest. My mother pointed out an army truck
with a khaki-covered canvas tarp over the back on the
beginning of that strip, and she said something critical
and worried-sounding about the damage a new road
might do. We were about to leave in a few days. 6:24 AM

I can imagine the high household dependency on
electronica. I understand it well for those of us who
live alone, but it saddens me to hear about it among

families. Keep persisting with your mother. I need to force myself to turn off my computer and phone on some evenings when Aijaz is away and I am alone, to paint and listen to music or even fold laundry and go to bed early. Which I did last night. It's the first time that I have woken up feeling rested in many days. 6:40 AM

Speaking of anti-Saudi politics, a few years ago it struck me that both Saudi and Israeli regimes deserve to be jointly boycotted. To be spoken of everywhere as twin entities. Yoked together. 6:41 AM

Only now is the extent of their ally-ship becoming mainstream news. 7:46 AM

I just heard an eerie rustling sound and looked out my window: snow! 9:51 AM

Barf-e-nau uftaad sadd mubarakbaad! 11:26 PM

Kheili mamnun, Sumayya khanom (said the last, lonely, shivering birch leaf). 10:35 AM

2017-12-22

I have been thinking a lot about what you said in the summer – about your ambition to buy a plot of land and grow flowers. 12:02 PM

The sun has come out today and some ancestral love of snowy forest and fresh air has crept into my blood. I climbed the hill at the park. 2:39 PM

2017-12-23

That terrifying beauty, typical Vancouver on the odd day, regardless of summer or winter. It made you pine for love. It disarmed you to the point of incapacitation. How many times I have felt paralyzed by that stark blue of Vancouver! 5:05 PM

The solstice brought a mildly lovely sunshine here, too, in Srinagar. But this is home. Vancouver was livelihood. 5:07 PM

> I hate the stark sunny blue, there were a few days in October when the glare was almost vicious. It was disturbing – as if premonition of a future post-apocalyptic desert – 10:53 AM

> Yesterday's light was gentler, and I enjoyed crunching through the snow in Aijaz's borrowed snow boots. He defiantly skipped the last day of school. I played hooky from work. 10:55 AM

2017-12-24

A celebration of the ombre effect in Naseem Bagh just now:

> Photo of a winter forest with a multi-hued sky backdrop. 5:59 PM

Fifth Rabi' al-Thani. 6:01 PM

> Ahhh. The ombre effect! Thank you – these are elating. The glorious height of the trees! 9:33 AM

2017-12-31

> Tonight I am resisting (though I am as sorely tempted as everyone else) the pull to draw any meaningful conclusions from the appearance of linear progression which is imparted by a new calendar year. The longer I go on the more I see it as my job – as reader, rememberer, and writer of poetry – indeed, my duty and possibly calling – to question our ways of measuring time and our obedience to its apparent demands. 7:50 PM

> I am not thrilled to find that I, too, very soon, will be another year older. 7:51 PM

2018-01-05

Salam new year nonetheless, dear Rahat. The older, the dearer, my late grandmother used to say.

I have been high on Urdu ghazals over the last few days. On poets I haven't heard of before, and on pairs of almost parallel lines, the jarring symmetry and counterpoint of the first and the second misra. It is too easy to lose oneself in this cosmos.

Your observation on the arbitrary tyranny of the Gregorian calendar has had me thinking of, and possibly resisting with you in spirit, the universal absence implicit in this linearity. 11:58 PM

On my ride back from work today I was reading Abdul Ahad Saaz, someone I had never heard of before … 11:59 PM

Who seems to be a serious shaa'ir of the ghazal … 11:59 PM

2018-01-06

And terribly underappreciated. 12:00 AM

As are the majority of the language and eloquence-rich urban Muslims of India. 12:00 AM

This shi'r reminded me of your resistance to the standards of timekeeping and had me thinking of more "organic" alternatives. 12:02 AM

زماں پیماں یہی مقیاسِ دِل تھا
مگر اب اُس کا پارہ مر رہا ہے

12:02 AM

I am very literally reading it as:

My heart was the gauge with which I used to measure / keep time
And now the mercury in it is dying.

12:03 AM

"Miqyās" is such a rich word. 12:04 AM

It reminds me of a beer mug and a barometer at the same time. 12:05 AM

As well as the measuring utensil that Yūsuf hid in his brother's backpack to charge him of theft so he could get him to stay with him. 12:07 AM

A rather rambling train of thought. 12:07 AM

And to think of how the rhythm of the heart as an organic timekeeper has been disrupted, perhaps impaired, by the perfect tick-tock of the sexagesimal system. 12:10 AM

I would like to regain part of that innate ability to keep time with my heart. 12:11 AM

But I need to get to work at the latest by 10:15 a.m. and I must clock in with my biometric. 12:12 AM

The laser flashes into my iris from a sinister aperture, and then a simulated feminine voice thanks me, and I instinctually tell her, "You're welcome." 12:13 AM

2018-01-05

Thank you for this. I have been quite sick since the night before yesterday and receiving this string of messages in Urdu poetry is like you visiting me in person. 11:15 AM

You know, in *The Ministry of Utmost Happiness*, one of the characters, a doctor in the Daryaganj neighbourhood behind the Jama Masjid in Delhi (where I visited Ghalib's haveli), believes in prescribing shi'r along with medication. He believes in the healing power of Urdu poetry. 11:20 AM

2018-01-06

Are you reading the ghazals of these new / unknown poets online? 11:21 AM

2018-01-05

My neighbour just knocked on my door. Yesterday I texted her with a desperately bad headache and she left me a bottle of ibuprofen outside my door. Just now she gave me homemade noodles cooked with greens, what marvellous kindness. 11:29 AM

Thank you for the interpretation of miqyās. 6:05 PM

You know, we need good tools of measurement for the things we value. 6:06 PM

I have been thinking a lot about this as a feminist principle. To fight capitalism, we need a proper sense of the value of things which are fundamental to life and abundance. Things like health and education and infant mortality are used as measures of success for nations. Some deeper social value should likewise be attached to women's experiences of bodily and moral autonomy. Gender equality must be embodied, not only legislated. 6:14 PM

2018-01-11

Salam Rahat. I am leaving for work. Parts of the lake's surface are frozen. It is bitterly cold. No news of snow yet. Please make du'ā. 8:15 AM

2018-01-10

> Done, with all my heart. 🖤 7:49 PM

2018-01-11

> Sumayya, my mother will be flying to Delhi in
> February. She'll be there until March 10. Would you
> consider visiting her? Maybe she will decide to go
> to Srinagar as well, but it has been minus thirty in
> Ottawa, so she needs to warm up, too. 9:29 AM

2018-01-12

Rahat, that will be a nice opportunity to meet your
mum. I can try to get a few days off work. 7:51 AM

> Salam dear Sumayya. I just read a critical piece
> in *The Wire* about the Aadhaar card and I
> immediately remembered your message. 5:10 PM

> It was written by some ex-intelligence (RAW?)
> official. It made my head spin. 5:12 PM

2018-02-01

> Dear Sumayya, we seem to have made it into
> February. It has rained incessantly, almost every
> single day, and we have reached that stage of being
> resigned to cold and wet existential conditions. I
> hope you and your family are all right. 12:05 PM

> About ten days ago, while I was out looking for a gift for
> a friend, I found an old brass vase and liked its shape
> and etched pattern. I bought it for myself. I then bought
> a bunch of carnation buds from the supermarket nearest
> my house. On the next evening, they bloomed. 12:10 PM

> Aijaz carried the vase out to the living room to take a
> photo. Under the foot of the vase, someone has engraved
> "INDIA." I have to say I feel that the vase is truly
> named, while the nation-state lies to itself. 12:13 PM

My mother has arrived in Delhi and is
seriously applying herself to appreciating its
rich and vibrant culture as you can see:

Video of a young man slumped in the street, mournfully singing in
Hindi / Urdu, until an irate passerby curses him for making such a racket
and tosses a plastic jug at him. The singer's refrain can be understood
in two different ways: "lautaado," relieve me (of some burden, implied
emotional pain, usually unrequited love) or "lotaa do," give me a lota
(water jug traditionally used throughout the subcontinent to wash with
after using the toilet). 7:55 PM

Maybe there is hope for me and Aijaz:

Link to an article about a new Kashmiri book intended to teach diasporic
children some Kashmiri vocabulary. 3:26 PM

I have been ill the last several days, and today the
sunlight glittered on snow. It has been a strange winter.
Time stretches out in all directions. It's never one
linear movement. I feel like I may be on the cusp of
change – there are days when all I can see, the only true
thing, is the material evidence of my suspended life
(especially this apartment, my ill-gotten gains on stolen
land; all the furniture I would like to drag out into the
alley and set fire to). But on other days, I'm sustained
by new connections and unexpected possibilities
over distances and across time zones. 5:36 PM

Dear Sumayya, how are you? I read last night that schools and colleges have been closed. And on Twitter I saw a photo of a group of Kashmiri men and women standing together for prayers in the woods at a burial ground; they were all wearing pherans except for one young man in jeans. I kept gazing at the range of colours in their clothing, from sombre to bright. 7:40 AM

2018-04-18

Salam and much love from Ottawa. I have been with my mother for two weeks. Flying back to my boy tomorrow. We went to Toronto and met Idrisa Pandit, who teaches at the University of Waterloo. She gave a talk about the last seventy-one years of Kashmiri history. 8:39 AM

Her talk ran long and its contents were news to many of the concerned citizenry of the mostly Muslim-diasporic audience. 8:40 AM

When it ended, I had to fight off the eager crowd to introduce myself and ask for her email address before we had to run to catch our bus and train. 8:53 AM

2018-04-19

Dear Rahat, salam and love from Kashmir. I do not really have a tangible reason for disappearing over the past few months; I guess I have been a little underwhelmed and feeling quite numb. My preoccupation with livelihood and the struggle to stay whole within the extensive labyrinth of patriarchal-imperialist soul crushers keeps me on the edge of being drained and needing to recharge. The need to connect with those who help me find sense – and power – through a return to shared meanings has often overwhelmed me to the point of paralysis. But in any case, I do not want to offer excuses. I am just left simultaneously ashamed and humbled by your presence in my "community." Thank you for being my community; and I am grateful to be among your "ahl." 11:35 PM

I haven't much to report on your Kashmir that you may not already have heard of and read about in the news. 11:36 PM

My little brother's wedding is in June / July this year and I find myself participating in the preparations with an intensity I no longer thought I could muster. 11:37 PM

My family and I would be so very, very happy if you and your mum and Aijaz could join us for the wedding. 11:38 PM

If you're planning to be around Kmr / India anytime during this year, please try to schedule it around end of June / first week of July. 11:39 PM

I hope you will let me know if this may be possible. 11:43 PM

2018-04-29

> I am working on it, dear Sumayya. I am sorry for the slow reply. This essay I am writing is extra gruelling, for some reason. It's due tomorrow and I am locked in an arm wrestle with it and I need to win. 3:54 PM
>
> I am also wondering how I am going to get through Ramadan in the concrete grid. 3:55 PM
>
> I'm at a low ebb just now. 3:55 PM
>
> Will be in touch in another week. 3:56 PM

2018-05-03

Dear Rahat, I hope you won. 9:05 PM

Yesterday someone told my mother that flowers had bloomed over her mother's grave. This is the first spring, and these the first flowers, since her death last year. My mother spent the entire day today at the graveyard. 9:08 PM

Dear Rahat, there is so much despair! A young boy named
Basim Aijaz was crushed by an army vehicle in the heart
of the city yesterday. And three to four young men are
killed each day. Then, Mohammad Rafi Bhat, a young
assistant professor of sociology at the University of Kashmir,
disappeared eight days ago and was killed today. There is no
line between mourning and getting on with life. Preparations
for my brother's wedding are the main preoccupation of
the family these days – it is the biggest event in the family,
since neither mine not my other brother's wedding were
proper Kashmiri affairs. My mother cried yesterday and said
we shouldn't illuminate the house with fairy lights on the
wedding – as Kashmiris routinely do – seeing the haalaat.
Haalaat is such an all-encompassing term in Koshur – and it
signifies so much shared meaning and shared trauma. 9:30 PM

I wish you relative peace in your corner of the world. It must
be superbly sunny in early May in Vancouver. Please give
my salam to Wreck Beach when – if – you ever go there.
I have spent many, many lonely hours there. 9:32 PM

> Carried these messages in my heart all day
> today, everywhere I went. 7:20 PM

2018-05-07

A Call to Arms

Somewhere along be-coming, we leave
Freedom
Be-holden to history

But apart from civilizational table talk, we walk
The tightrope between East and West
You the clown and I
Juggler reincarnate
Have you not documented each instance
Of me undressing; you
Have posed for me in various
States of Unrest.

Ah, un-rest!
That word they used for the summers
Of 2008, 2009, 2010, 2012
Settled in the bones of our marriage
In the sly dilemma
Between the wall and the headboard

So history, as it be-comes, comes
Undone;
My mother's Persian carpet – a mother-to-daughter heirloom – snags on
    a Something
And she remembers everything her mother ever said, all at once,

"Why is everything on fire?" she'd constantly ask on her deathbed,
Until my mother read her Hafez of Shiraz;
And her mother – contrapuntal by birth – hummed a Kashmiri wedding
    song
That always begins in Shiraz.

Our wedding, you'll remember,
Was a celebration of symbols
And after all was said and done
(And more was said than done)
It took me an entire winter
To fold my trousseau of words
Back alphabetically

But love, as you never quite got to see,
Always was a call to arms
So somewhere along the road to freedom, we tied
Knots to the mouth of the rifle
To keep track of the anniversary

10:32 AM

This is filled with the things of my own heart,
Sumayya – I just wrote about Said's explication
of contrapuntal reading in that essay I have
finally wrestled into submission. 8:57 PM

But even that line – "contrapuntal by birth" – is not the
reason that is my favourite verse in this poem – 8:58 PM

It's the whole verse. It's like a room filled
with things and people I love. 8:59 PM

2018-05-17

Dear Sumayya, I have made the masala with onions,
fennel, salt, chili powder, garlic, and ginger, and half a
bottle of strained tomatoes. I am about to add it to the
cooked chopped spinach and kale, and then I will crush
some fenugreek and add it to the saag. I will leave it to
simmer. I will ponder my options. What is the name of
the energy unleashed in Ramadan? What strength wakes
up in us and what forgotten gifts lie asleep. 4:37 PM

2018-05-27

Last night I was reminded of your line, "I am grateful
to be among your 'ahl.'" I return the same gratitude to
you as I attended an iftar party last night where I found
myself literally in the company of your "ahl" – more
prosaically, your second cousin Hamzah. 10:16 PM

Such a rare thing – to meet another Kashmiri in
Vancouver – of course, you were the first and last
Kashmiri I met here. My unexpected meeting with
Hamzah allowed me the rare feeling of being at
home, as the more superficial chatter swirled around
us among many grown-up children of Pakistanis,
Sri Lankans, Egyptians, and others who don't know
what we are living through. Being at home, for
me, now means being with the people with whom
I am able to talk about real things. 10:23 PM

2018-05-28

I am so happy you finally met Hamzah. 10:54 AM

2018-05-30

Dear Rahat, I am tired. I am drowning in toxicity. I haven't read anything meaningful in months. I need a refuge.

I ask you to make du'ā for me, for me to be restored to wholeness, for the darknesses to be lifted, for the knots to be resolved, for rizq to be uncomplicated. Please. 3:58 AM

2018-05-29

Always. 3:28 PM

If there is anything I can do, I also pray you tell me what it is. 3:29 PM

I've been grappling with the fact that the fascism-driven occupation will take multiple generations to dismantle. 3:31 PM

And I need to feel that I am doing anything to defy it with whatever strength I can give. 3:32 PM

Could travel be a possible practical step for you in the near future? 3:35 PM

2018-05-30

The truth is that I want to leave. Not just travel. 4:05 AM

But to leave and never have to return. 4:06 AM

2018-05-29

I know that exact "never." 3:37 PM

Almost too intimately. 3:37 PM

2018-05-30

Over the last few months I have developed an intense yearning for Malaysia. I want to make a pilgrimage. 4:07 AM

2018-05-29

Oh my goodness, I had the thought in my mind before you typed it! 3:37 PM

Malaysia, I mean. 3:37 PM

2018-05-30

Rahat, let us meet in KL as soon as we both can. 4:07 AM

2018-05-29

> Did you know that I include Terengganu
> Beach in my prayers? 3:38 PM

2018-05-30

I did not know! I have some idea that Malaysia
has been special to you. 4:08 AM

2018-05-29

> I think it's brilliant – I love the idea of meeting you in KL.
>
> I really wanted to come to Kashmir, Sumayya. I want
> to come. I have some travel money set aside. But as
> every day brings more news of injustice and death, I
> feel as if my own spirit is being slowly choked in the
> concertina wire of the murderous occupation. 3:42 PM
>
> In August it will be twenty years since
> I was in Srinagar. 3:43 PM
>
> Although there are days when I feel like I
> could face anything on my own – if I left
> Aijaz here for the summer. 3:44 PM
>
> (Which is what he wants me to do.) 3:45 PM

2018-05-30

If we meet in Srinagar that will heal
parts of the city for me. 4:16 AM

And if we meet in KL that will heal other parts of me. 4:17 AM

Parts that are dying in me. 4:17 PM

Either way I will benefit from meeting you. 4:17 AM

2018-05-29

> I know what you mean. 3:47 PM
>
> Yes, I think the planet needs the unleashed force of
> us being in the same city somewhere. 3:48 PM

2018-05-30

Or maybe the intense peace of it. 4:19 AM

Let us plan for this international peace conference
and maybe make it an annual event. 4:20 AM

2018-05-29

> I was talking to a writing mentor on Friday night – a
> wise and gentle elder spirit. I confided in her about
> my yearning to return to Kashmir. She said that she
> thinks I should make that a priority. She said that on
> returning, I will know what I need to do next. 3:51 PM

> This was my prayer last night and this morning:
> Let the bones in the hands of all oppressors turn
> to water wherever they lift them with the intent to
> do harm, whenever they raise them in fists or reach
> for guns. Let the bones in the hands of tyrants
> defy them by turning to water and draining them
> of all power to cause harm. Ameen. 4:00 PM

2018-05-30

Ameen. 5:01 AM

2018-06-09

> Dearest Sumayya, how are you? My ticket is booked
> to Delhi. Delhi door ast, as the old strategists and
> connivers of empire once said. I will book a flight
> through to SXR when my visa comes through. 8:27 PM

> Tell me what to bring and how to prepare myself. 8:29 PM

2018-06-10

RAHAT! 9:00 AM

You're coming. 9:00 AM

The most beautiful of surprises. 9:00 AM

This will take me a while to process. 9:01 AM

2018-06-09

> Me too. Inshallah. Indeed. 8:31 PM

2018-06-10

Do you know where you will be staying in Srinagar? 9:19 AM

2018-06-09

> Wherever my aunts decide to put me. When my mother
> comes, we may take a week in a houseboat. My cousin
> will be getting married in Wazir Bagh on August 1 and
> my aunt & uncle may have other guests coming. 8:55 PM

2018-06-14

> Found this. Me getting a henna treatment
> in the back garden at my grandparents'
> house. Wazir Bagh. Late August 1998:

Photo of Rahat Kurd getting a henna treatment, with members of her family. 10:58 AM

> With my mother in purple, looking on. 10:59 AM

2018-06-15

Wow! 8:25 AM

2018-06-16

Eid Mubarak, dear Rahat. 10:08 AM

2018-06-15

> Eid said, dear Sumayya. Health and strength
> and justice restored to you. 9:41 PM

2018-06-16

Ameen. 10:11 AM

2018-07-03

Dear Sumayya, how are you? How is your family? Did your brother's marriage proceed smoothly? I hope it did and that you all found some strength and hope in the event. I have to tell you that my visa application was rejected; the regime requires more money and hurdle-jumping from those of us who wish to visit Kashmir. I have to re-strategize. I will keep you posted. Sending love. 12:22 AM

2018-07-15

Inshallah, I will be in Srinagar from July 30–August 28. 4:39 PM

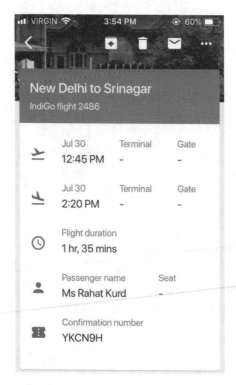

Your IndiGo Itinerary - YKCN9H

2018-07-16

Dear Rahat, inshallah! Thank you for giving me
such beautiful news. I will be in a constant state
of prayer until you land, inshallah. 10:17 AM

2018-07-15

I am so happy to share this happiness with you.
I have just come back from Kitsilano Beach ...
there was a new moon above a pink-streaked
sky. I'm giving thanks tonight. 9:50 PM

2018-07-17

I would like you to please tell me what I can
bring for you. Are there any books you want?
I've been reading Anna Akhmatova. 1:49 PM

Her writing strikes the satisfying balance between
emotional resonance and political urgency. She and
Cavafy are so pithy on the topic of the city ... each of them
lived in truly great cities (Saint Petersburg and Alexandria
respectively) in the old sense of the word. They make me
feel better about inhabiting this frontier town. 1:53 PM

The Akhmatova is a tiny, pocket-sized
thing – I will bring it for you. 1:55 PM

2018-07-18

Akhmatova would be lovely! Thank you. 7:32 AM

PART THREE

In Kashmir,
with Akhmatova and
Antihistamines

WELCOME TO PARADISE flashes in green LED lights on a large screen suspended from the Srinagar Airport Arrivals ceiling. Not only does the garish display kill any weary traveller's hope of a quiet, understated arrival, it shuts out all other possible conclusions as to what arrival means. "Paradise" has been triumphantly shoved in my face before I can even get off the escalator and claim my luggage.

After making me fill out a foreign visitor's form with my passport and visa details, explanation of what I do for a living, and why I have come to Jammu & Kashmir (ampersand theirs), officials will release me from SXR into the bright and dusty Srinagar air. A line of cab drivers will watch me make my way to where my mother waves when she sees it's really me. We roll my suitcase through a gap in a fence to a VIP parking lot where the loaned-by-a-generous-friend car and driver are waiting. Then we have our own smaller, private moment of triumph – that we have claimed a few weeks together in the only place where the word home has never felt contingent or temporary.

Later the same afternoon, one of the officials from the Foreign Visitors' desk will call my cousin at the number I was required to provide on the form, to verify that I am the person I have claimed. "Is she really a writer?" they will ask her. "Is it true she just came to Kashmir to attend your wedding?"

Dear Sumayya, I woke up about an hour ago, the first rising of the nearest muezzin's voice simultaneously rousing indignant howls and whines among the dogs asleep in the nearby alley. Our heads (I am sleeping in the same bed as my mother) lie close to the wall that abuts the T-intersection of two narrow lanes that lead to the front door of the house.

I'm not letting it get to me yet – the amount of time I've been gone. The obvious despoilment of army bunkers and barbed wire cannily scaled back from their overwhelming presence on every city block when I was here last. The matter-of-fact way my aunts discuss how tonight's evening traffic might be affected by "the handing over of the body" – a young man the soldiers killed a month ago – to his family in Baramulla. They refer to the dead boy as a militant, and my mind registers the *glib*, clearly self-protective way everyone uses the term with the same clinical rigour it notes the supreme persistence of beauty all around me. The undeterred carrying-on-ness of leaves glittering in the sun and the rich chorus of birds who took up their cue as soon as the hour-long recitation of post-Fajr zikr over the mosque loudspeakers fell silent. The fairy lights announcing my cousin's wedding are warm and bright in the blue dawn, cascading over the cream-coloured walls of the house my grandfather built sixty years ago.

Kashmir's life-force and sovereignty remind me who I am and what I must do. After my long exile, after dwelling too long in states of loss, I feel as if I have just stepped effortlessly into my inheritance.

2018-08-04

I'm finally online, dear Sumayya. We are going to the walima late this evening and then I think we will be done with the formal wedding events. Please God. 3:43 PM

Ha ha, the wedding seems to have overwhelmed you. 4:00 PM

Me resolute in a simple cotton kurta. 4:02 PM

I have to iron a sari before long and I'm not looking forward to it. 4:02 PM

Rocking the henna. 4:03 PM

Yes. It was a late-night mehndi session. I was
falling asleep then, but now I regret not getting
it on both sides of my hands, to look like
gloves. The effect is very striking. 4:08 PM

2018-08-06

Good morning. I'm back online, and free today, like the
entire city, hoping to talk to you and to see you soon. I
woke up with some lines in my head – I think they're
Shahid's – about "a city that is always leaving" – 8:10 AM

2018-08-07

Salam Rahat, the city just did feel as if it was leaving.
I hope the situation in Rajbagh is under control,
it is usually one of the first to flood. 10:03 AM

I am on my way to work right now. 10:05 AM

I am free in the evenings, please let me know if you can
spare an evening and what you'd like to do. 10:06 AM

Have you been up the Shankaracharya Hill? 10:06 AM

I have been thinking of a trek there on Sunday. 10:07 AM

I haven't really been anywhere yet. 10:07 AM

That sounds great. 10:07 AM

Great, inshallah. There is also an amazing trek
and lookout point just outside of Srinagar that
we can go to if weather permits. 10:08 AM

It gives you an unobstructed view of Dal and most
of the eastern city and Zabarwan. 10:09 AM

I can't wait. The rain will only let up on Friday
night, according to the forecast. I am chagrined
to find myself in this rain with not a single piece
of the equipment I use almost daily in Vancouver.
No boots no jacket no umbrella … 10:10 AM

I will probably get some writing done, though. 10:10 AM

With some nadeir monje on the side, yes. 😄 10:11 AM

We can drive around a little in the rain in the evenings if
you find yourself inclined and need a break. 10:13 AM

> Yes, if roads aren't flooded, let's do that. 10:14 AM

I think you must have been able to check
out Zero Bridge, though? 10:14 AM

> Not yet. We did go for a walk on the Bund one early
> cool morning last week, and my mum and her younger
> brother (who lives in Australia) pointed out their routes
> to school and where their friends lived and where they
> remembered the best windfall from fruit trees. I saw
> the newish large-ish mosque, the Goodfellas café, and
> the steps leading down to Lambert Lane. 10:18 AM

> Nothing was open, though ... 10:19 AM

> And it was difficult to cope with how neglected
> such a beautiful riverfront has become, knowing
> how it was before and could be again. 10:21 AM

True, most of the memoried parts of the city are now what
I think is the "dilapidoria." The parts that are "salvaged"
are courtesy of corporate interests, mostly J&K Bank.
And that, of course, changes everything. 10:24 AM

RAHAT TRAVEL DIARY
2018-08-07

> The communal breakfast is possibly one of my
> foundational memories: my standard measure of
> unconditional belonging. To come home to Srinagar is to
> fall into the communal breakfast routine, no questions
> or debate. We eat together, uncles and aunts, cousins and
> siblings sitting cross-legged on the floor around a floor
> cloth, for every meal, as a matter of course, but for some
> reason, breakfast is when I cherish the collective most. In
> Srinagar I realize that my Vancouver habit of rising half
> an hour earlier than my son on school mornings, to wash
> and cut up some fruit and make eggs or porridge, mark an
> attempt that's either resignedly pervaded by, or an attempt

to compensate for, my consciousness that something will always be missing – vitally, that people are missing.

Yesterday, as soon as I was awake and dressed, I laced up my running shoes and walked with my uncle Kabir down one of Wazir Bagh's old alleys to the kaandar, the local bread maker. The doors of the houses in the dusty narrow lane were variously old and ornate, the light was bright, and the day was already very hot at 8 a.m. It was the second day of a two-day strike in Srinagar, and – as the deserted autorickshaw parked nearby confirmed – the neighbourhood bakers were the only people going to work. The baker in a white skull cap rapidly pressed indentations with his fingertips into every round of flattened dough he then slapped onto the inside wall of the open tandoor next to him. Another baker lifted the baked rounds out of the oven with tongs;

a third accepted money from the waiting customers as he handed them stacks of the finished tsauch through the open window of the shop. I have frequently craved this bread during my twenty years away from Kashmir. The closest thing I've found are fresh sesame bagels from St-Viateur Bagel in Montréal; two years ago I stood in a friend's kitchen in the Plateau eating one out of a paper bag at eleven o'clock on a freezing cold night, hungry less for calories than a sense-memory of love.

Later in the afternoon the news broke that the supreme court had opted to postpone its decision on the legal status of Kashmir, specifically the long-standing article 35A restricting the purchase of property in the state to Kashmiris only, a concession granted to Kashmir in exchange for remaining under Indian rule (and used as an excuse to postpone the UN plebiscite),

COMPLETE STRIKE

ON 5TH AND 6TH AUGUST

AGAINST

ABROGATION OF

ARTICLE

35-A

WE WILL SACRIFICE OURSELVES FOR OUR RIGHTS.

ALL KASHMIR AUTO RICKSHAW DRIVERS ASSOCIATION

which right-wing Indian nationalist groups have now vindictively positioned in their crosshairs. The postponement meant that Kashmiri trade unions and other groups could end their strike, a temporary reprieve – another of the ill-gotten gains of life under occupation. At night the skies flashed and rumbled with lightning and thunder for nearly an hour before rain – my persistent, unwanted hamsafar – fell. This morning we ate our tsauch and drank our chai in the combined gloom of heavy rains and power failure (internet works though: yay). My aunts look worriedly at the sky while my cousins determinedly turn their backs to it, refusing to believe another deluge could be coming, as if from loyalty to their city. I don't want to think about the Hunter boots or umbrellas I left in Vancouver. I want this rain to wash the air clear of smog so I can photograph the blue Himalayas properly. I haven't really been able to see them yet.

2018-08-08

Internet still miraculously working. You can call either me or my mum when you arrive. 6:22 PM

The sun is out. 😎 6:23 PM

I just got home. 6:26 PM

I will leave in half an hour, inshallah. 6:27 PM

Waiting for my dad to be back. 6:27 PM

Okay, inshallah. 🙂 6:27 PM

Leaving now. 7:11 AM

RAHAT TRAVEL DIARY
2018-08-09

Last night I met Sumayya at nearly eight o'clock, in front of the Pine Spring Hotel. We drove close to the south end of Zero Bridge, then walked across amid perhaps a few dozen nighttime visitors. The night was clear and the bridge, ornately made of very new timber, was indeed designed to charm the public into lingering. Sumayya pointed out signs marking state and corporate sponsorship of what she called "this overdetermined public destination." As we walked across the bridge, past the Bund, and up to Residency Road, she told me she had recently considered becoming a historic walking tour guide but in the end couldn't accept the tourism-driven erasure of Srinagar's lived reality: occupation, struggle, pollution, venality.

After doubling back to the south end of the bridge, we sat down on the rooftop patio of a restaurant shaped very like a replica toy houseboat we brought back from our visit in 1979. I gazed at the menu and named things I wished to eat; Sumayya spoke in a commandingly elegant Kashmiri to the young man who had come to take our order. His movements were careful and his manner deferential, only taking exception to our insistence that hot water necessarily meant *boiled* water. But the food he brought out was hot, fresh, flavourful, and delicious. As we sat and talked, I could look out over the river, which remained itself in the night. The feeling I have looking at the river, of something implacably vital, beside which I'm restored to proper insignificance.

Rahat, the Akhmatova is power-packed! And the notebook is lovely. Thank you. Yesterday evening will stay with me for many years to come. 11:10 AM

Salam Sumayya. I am still absorbing all the things you said. Especially that you had not been out at night with a friend since you had come back to Srinagar. 11:28 AM

I am spending some time with my aunt Tasneem today for all clothes-related matters (laundry and shopping). I've also been enjoying getting to know my two cousins' young daughters (they have two each; eighteen & thirteen, and eight & three months). It has been delightful. But I want some mountains and forest time & looking forward to our next plan. 11:45 AM

I knew you would find a kindred
voice in Akhmatova. 12:37 PM

2018-08-10

Salam Rahat, we have this Sunday (Aug. 12)
and then Wednesday (Aug. 15) to make use of.
Aug. 15 will be hartal, though, but I want to know
how you'd prefer to spend the time. 9:41 AM

Wa salam. Can we plan to go on the trek you mentioned
earlier – with the view of Dal and Zabarwan? Also,
how is your Saturday afternoon? A school-days
friend of my mother's is organizing a lunch on the
Bund. She was friends with Shahid and may be
able to take us to visit his father. I will keep you
posted but I'd love for you to join us. 9:48 AM

Re: the trek for Sunday the twelfth would be great. 9:49 PM

We also need to have a bookstore and coffee
hangout when it's not hartal. 9:49 PM

But when you have time. 9:50 AM

2018-08-11

You must be at work today. I hope all is well. The
daytime heat on the streets is intense in a way
I don't remember in Kashmir – 10:58 AM

Salam Rahat, yes, I am at work. I would have loved to attend
the lunch today, but it is unlikely I can make it. 11:31 AM

May I make a suggestion regarding the
trek and bookstore stroll? 11:32 AM

Sure. 11:32 AM

Since Aug. 15 is hartal, it is easier to fit in the trek since we
don't need anything to be open; we should be able to take
my car to the hill on the city outskirts without incident,
inshallah, and that way Aug. 15 will be utilized (unless
you already have a different plan for the day). We could
do the bookstores on Sunday (the twelfth). 11:34 AM

I like that idea. 11:34 AM

Since hopefully transport and everything will be open. 11:34 AM

Disclaimer about bookstores, though ... 11:34 AM

Srinagar is not a bookstore city. 11:35 AM

There used to be a Kashmir Book Shop on Residency Road. Where I bought my first Shahid in 2001. It is now replaced by a so-called gift shop. Which sells shiny stuff to teenagers. 11:35 AM

The main one now is Gulshan. We'll go there, inshallah. And I have a couple of old, rather decrepit bookstores in mind. Otherwise it's dismal. 11:36 AM

There's a swanky café / burger joint called Books & Bricks nearby, close to where you live. The idea is to have books (mostly bestsellers like Paolo Coelho 😄 😄) on the shelves high above while teenagers eat burgers and drink milkshakes. 11:38 AM

The books are there for ambience. 11:39 AM

Just preparing you for disappointment. 😄 😄 11:39 AM

Ugh re: selling shiny stuff to teenagers – not disappointed really, but it's like Chapters / Indigo all over again. I think Shahid may have actually mentioned the Kashmir Book Shop in a poem or in some notes. I have a collection of short stories translated from Urdu which I bought from there in 1998. I have witnessed the loss of many a bookstore in my time in Vancouver, too. 11:44 AM

Do you like picnics? 11:46 AM

If my aunts and cousins do get one organized for tomorrow as they have been hinting, I would like you to come with us. 11:47 AM

Also, I read the prose poem you posted on Facebook. We have to talk about your writing. 11:53 AM

It needs a proper literary home. 11:53 AM

Not the one provided by Zuckerberg. 11:54 AM

😂 😂 11:54 AM

Would love to talk to you about it. 11:55 AM

Inshallah. Tomorrow. 11:55 AM

Dear Sumayya, there has been no follow-up from the cousin who suggested or threatened picnic. Let's please make our own plans for tomorrow. 7:00 PM

2018-08-16

Dear Sumayya, I'm afraid I'm not any better this a.m. Headache and fever keep coming back. I feel so helpless. I will check in with you at around 1 p.m. 9:24 PM

Please get rested, Rahat. I will come see you today, inshallah. Let us not strain you. 9:51 PM

I would really appreciate that. I'm sorry for being such a feeble guest. 9:52 PM

You're home, Rahat. You need to be as comfortable as possible. 9:53 PM

I am still happy to be here, although my fevered brain went to work writing a feminist manifesto at Fajr this morning. They have the loudspeakers at a nearby mosque cranked to maximum. Some of the recitation was melodic, but most of these bros are just phoning it in. 9:55 PM

I mean, how is coughing and sniffing carelessly into the mic not insulting to God? 9:56 PM

They're getting into heaven by the sheer volume of their voice. 9:58 PM *LOL* LOL

2018-08-17

Rahat, is it okay if I visit around one? 10:30 AM

> I am having the most infuriating time with Google Maps. 11:29 AM

> Can I give the phone to my aunt and you talk to her? 11:30 AM

> She can direct you properly. 11:30 AM

Okay, I'll get there, and then give you a call. 11:31 AM

> Theek hai. 11:31 AM

> My mother has been telling her sisters that when I was pressuring her to book these travel plans with me, she was afraid I would get sick exactly in the manner that I have done. But I reply that I also got sick staying put in Vancouver – several times last winter, in fact. By the way, dear Sumayya – thank you for the fruit. 😊 6:05 PM

2018-08-18

It is sometimes still quite unreal when I think that you're actually here. We are in the same city. You're forty minutes away. Forty minutes and daily routines. 8:13 AM

> My fever made it seem unreal, even when you were sitting here yesterday.

> After you left, I slept again. In the evening we were invited to the home of Gazala, one of my aunt's nieces. Her cooking was just incredible. I think I started to revive from the fragrance of the saag alone. The "head trapped in tunnel" feeling has lifted. 9:32 AM

2018-08-19

> Salam – hope you're well. My mother and aunt are leaving Srinagar this morning – many family & friends pressed them to stay longer, but changing tickets in the peak summer season is impossible. 8:17 AM

> I'm so sorry I wasn't able to bring them to meet your mother as well. 9:03 AM

Salam Rahat. I am under a paralyzing bout of migraine since yesterday evening. 1:31 PM

Oh no. Sorry to hear that. 1:33 PM

The heat is overpowering, I am sitting with an ice pack on my neck with the AC on full blast. 1:34 PM

Hope the ice pack is helping you. 1:36 PM

What a sad pair we are. 1:36 PM

I actually talked to my headache and tried to reason with it to leave me. 1:38 PM

It doesn't seem to be the kind to listen. 1:38 PM

It needs some sort of exorcistic ritual. 1:42 PM

How are you? I woke up this morning thinking about zombies. 7:46 PM

It is going to take me a while to work through what zombies might possibly have to do with being in SXR. 7:47 PM

It's a pleasant evening now of course. I need to get over being intimidated to go out by myself. 7:49 PM

Delhi was bad for my morale in this regard. 7:50 PM

I did get sleep, and sorry I missed your call! An uncle in the family just passed away and we're all here now. The burial and everything will take until after Isha.

Have you heard from your mother? I hope the journey is not straining them too much.

I feel the loss of another day I could have spent with you.

Yesterday afternoon I got ambushed by a meeting with a "prospective" that some family friends had arranged. The meeting was dispiriting, not unexpectedly so. Thankfully, it's worn off pretty quickly. 8:44 PM

It's so strange to me that you are still being put through these scenes. 9:31 PM

I've just been doing some writing. My brain is making up for the rest of my body's inactivity. 9:33 PM

I'm trying to keep the thought of how soon I'm leaving here at bay. 9:33 PM

Sorry for the disjointed thoughts. Yes, my mother and aunt are all right; we have been texting back and forth since they got to Delhi and met my cousin Imran for a few hours; they will board their flight to Toronto soon.

I walked around my aunt's garden when the sun went down and I think that is prompting all the ideas of writing and zombies and so forth. 9:36 PM

My cousin's little eight-year-old daughter was unhappy with me for leaving Wazir Bagh a few hours after my mother's departure, but we will see each other on Eid, it was decided. 9:39 PM

I'm so sorry about the loss of your uncle. I think you saw the mourners' tent which was put up in T Auntie's garden on Friday when you visited. 9:55 PM

My aunt was explaining the mourning customs to me, including the wailing. 9:56 PM

On Saturday I was very struck by the sound of the women's wailing, because it followed so quickly after my complaints about men taking up all the aural space with azaan and qirat. 9:58 PM

This is all me not having swum or walked or run in a few weeks, so not being able to shut off my brain. 9:59 PM

Dear Sumayya, this morning the fajr azaan, prayers, and zikr were muffled by the T-shirt I had wrapped around my head before I slept, and as a result I rather enjoyed the qirat – the reciter sounded older and had more of the local melancholic Sufiyana style rather than the textbook pan-Islamic classical. Combined with the multilayered birdsong it was rather moving, especially during the call-and-response duas and zikr.

I got up and walked with my uncle to Jogger's Park, where he goes every morning at 6 a.m. We took several rounds of the park in the cool air and watched the sun come up over the mountains. It was a good moment.

I have a craving for fresh walnuts. Wondering if we can find some in the floating markets? 12:55 PM

Hi Rahat. Do you fancy that kulfi right now? 5:58 PM

Hi. How are you? Kulfi sounds lovely. 6:10 PM

I am just leaving from home. The traffic looks terrible. 6:12 PM

But hopefully I'll be there in an hour. Is that okay? 6:13 PM

That would be lovely. 6:13 PM

I'm at Tasneem Auntie's, as before. 6:13 PM

Okay. See you soon. 6:14 PM

Salam Rahat, here is just one of the cheesy stock Eid mubaraks I have received today on WhatsApp from more than a dozen people who never speak to me:

Image of a cartoon sheep with a flower-like mandala body, a Santa hat on its head, Christmas-stocking-style boots on its feet, and multicoloured text reading "May Allah bless you with a 'beautiful feast of Sacrifice' on this auspicious day of Eid ul-Adha! Happy Bakra Eid." 11:02 AM

Salam Sumayya. That's impressive. I only received three or four such greetings. I am at my cousin's house now and I just sat through the worst azaan on record. 12:50 PM

I doubt that. 12:52 PM

Dude sounded like his guts were being slowly extracted by hand. Incompetent muezzins with poor to no vocal training are deeply offensive to my delicate tajwid-trained ears, as you know. 12:52 PM

I had a pleasant Eid namaz at the neighbourhood Salafi-educational complex. The lady next to me kindly pushed all her weight on me. 12:54 PM

And after the prayer was over, I turned to her and said Eid mubarak and leaned in for a hug. 12:55 PM

 12:55 PM

She pushed me away with both hands, disgusted. She pointed to my toes. And screamed, "WHAT ARE YOU WEARING?" 12:55 PM

"IS THAT NAIL PAINT?" 12:56 PM

I didn't really know what to say. I just looked at my toes. Then she gave her verdict that my prayer wasn't accepted. 12:56 PM

And that I contaminated her prayer as well. 12:57 PM

The last remaining Muslim cell in my body has now died. 1:00 PM

We need to make you a ta'weez against Salafis. 1:07 PM

I feel better about sleeping through prayers. 1:08 PM

Still at my cousin's. Just going over your e-cards again. The conflation of cute, fluffy, anthropomorphized sheep with some kind of deep religiosity in these Eid greetings is … really bizarre. The tackiness and decadence that a hyper-performative religiosity (and therefore a refusal to pay any serious attention to art history / principles) makes permissible. 11:36 PM

Eid ul Adha is a complicated holiday, although the
reasons for this have evolved over the course of my
life. I've nearly always fasted or been around people
fasting in Ramadan, so it's always been easy to feel
the anticipation and joy of Eid ul Fitr, but I've never
performed the Hajj; so the rationale for the feast of
sacrifice becomes abstract at the best of times. It marks
a physical pilgrimage and an ideal of the concept of
sacrifice older than Islam itself, rooted in the heavier
inherited monotheism of Abraham the Patriarch.

In Srinagar I've also learned I am not the only Muslim
woman who wakes up on Eid ul Adha with a lot of
complicated feelings or being tempted to ignore the
holiday altogether. Over kulfi faloodas last night,
Sumayya confided that she could not bear the thought
of the actual sheep-killing her family expected her
to take part in the next day. It's considered a social
responsibility (since much of the meat is distributed
to the needy) and therefore a sign of social prestige
as well. I had ventured a conversation with my own
aunt and uncle two nights before, telling them that
progressive Islamic scholars question whether in the
twenty-first century we really need to take the symbology
of the sacrifice quite so literally, given the negative
environmental impact of meat-heavy diets. At an Eid
sermon last year, I heard the argument that Muslims
need to frame animal stewardship practices with Islamic
ideals of justice and compassion, rather than assuming
ownership. My aunt and uncle listened quite patiently.

2018-08-26

I have asked my mother to accompany us. 1:12 PM

I hope you'll enjoy her company. 1:12 PM

Since I haven't been able to bring you home. 1:12 PM

> That will be nice. We're both keeping it in the family today. 1:13 PM

> I am really out of things as regards where to go. Uncle Zia took me to Badam Vaeri. 1:14 PM

Oh, you finally went there. 1:14 PM

> It was an unexpected breath of fresh air. 1:14 PM

> It was sad to see the state of Nigeen Lake, but you had prepared me for the corporate-sponsorship mood of the place. 1:16 PM

> Dear Sumayya, I hope you reach home quickly and feel better very soon. I forgot to give you back your scarf and also I forgot the lotus pods in the car. 9:22 PM

> Please eat them for me. Many thanks to you and to your mother as well, for your company today and for taking me to so many places. 9:32 PM

Video of nighttime row on Dal Lake, with Sumayya's mother's voice singing "Ye hawa, ye raat, ye chandni,"[5] as the full moon is reflected in the black waves.

> I am so happy with this video. Your mother's singing is exceptional, mashallah. 9:52 PM

2018-08-27

Thank you, Rahat. 8:29 PM

I just realized that tomorrow is the twenty-eighth. 8:31 PM

What time is your flight? 8:34 PM

> Everything I had planned to do today was cancelled due to closures and reports of disturbances and fear of further disturbances. 9:49 PM

> I packed and washed my hair and texted people. 9:53 PM

My flight is scheduled for 2:15 p.m. At the insistence of the driver, I will leave my aunt's place at 10 a.m. to avoid hordes of returning Hajjis. 10:04 PM

I am pretty sure this means I will be sitting in the airport for three hours tomorrow with no Wi-Fi. 10:06 PM

Today when I woke up, I felt such a deep dislike of the prospect of leaving. Even though the noise levels have been so formidable that I actually look forward to the frosty silence of Canadian nights. 10:46 PM

I was afraid yesterday when we were out that I was getting ill again, but the headache passed with steaming and so on. I'm really grateful to you for plotting the time we had so we could walk as much as possible. I will especially be thinking about that night shikara on Dal Lake for a long time. 10:55 PM

And eating kulfi in the open bus shelter. I really like the photo I took of you in blurred electric lights. 10:56 AM

2018-08-28

You must be getting ready to leave. 9:15 AM

We did not spend enough time together. 9:16 AM

The thought that I have been a lousy host will haunt me; I can only hope that we get another chance, several more opportunities to improve on this year, inshallah. The next time you visit I hope to have moved on to a more meaningful, more halal source of income. 9:20 AM

But alhamdulillah, I am thankful that we did experience some spaces and some times together in Srinagar. I can't shake off this persistent thought that in the spaces where we sat and talked, some kind of warping of time took place. 9:22 AM

It's the end of August, and this morning I heard the cicadas for the first time. I am on the way to work, there seems to be a cicada in every tree. 9:24 PM

Autumn's shrill call to prayer. 9:24 AM

When you're flying out of Srinagar, there's a wistful sense of non-return, which I hope you'll overcome. 9:26 AM

Yes. You know, this is exactly it. 9:55 AM

The thing I am telling myself is to remember the unexceptional nature of home, to resist the pull towards sentiment. 9:57 AM

And to remember its ordinariness. The autumnal turn in the weather and the light last night was remarkable. The way it arrived on time. Inexorably. 10:00 AM

I'm waiting for the cab driver now. 10:00 AM

I always resent autumn for what strikes me as its extreme punctuality. 10:01 AM

Please don't dwell on the things we weren't able to do this time – we were both under considerable physical constraints. If I had to get sick, perhaps it means I will have built up better immunity for next time. 10:04 AM

And please send me the poems we discussed. 10:05 AM

Finally: Don't hate, but you would always have a home with me if you could bring yourself to come to Vancouver. If it could possibly be useful to you work-wise or life-wise to have an interim there on your way somewhere else, don't rule it out. 10:12 AM

Please give my thanks and salams to your mother for her kindness. I'm looking forward to making kehwa with the zafran. (Shahid: "Saffron, my payment!") 10:15 AM

I hope you don't have to spend too long at the Delhi airport. 9:25 PM

Less than half an hour! I'm at my friend Reyhan's house for the next few days. 9:40 PM

Salam Rahat, how are you? We're just done with my cousin's wedding. It will take me tens of thousands of rupees worth of therapy to get over the trauma that being involved in a Kashmiri wedding takes. Especially with close family who insist on expressing how problematic your existence is. I am still dealing with migraine and haven't slept in three nights. I wish two people deciding to have socially sanctioned sex didn't have to inconvenience the entire world ... 11:06 AM

Khair, please tell me how you're doing. 11:10 AM

It seems like a distance dream when you were here. 11:10 AM

Hmmm. I wish I knew what to suggest that would end your three-day migraine and your mother's ten-year cough and my aunt's twenty-year asthma. Lack of sleep is an intolerable injustice.

Still. This made me laugh out loud: "I wish two people deciding to have socially sanctioned sex didn't have to inconvenience the entire world." 😂 11:20 AM

I have been taking antihistamines daily this week and am feeling restored to normalcy after all the sneezing and congestion. Also from being able to go out and see things and use my brain – Reyhan had cajoled me to give a talk at the college yesterday. There were maybe forty-five young women who showed up and we talked about the advantages and opportunities of living in a multilingual society. Several of them asked me afterwards for advice about writing. 11:26 AM

It's been pleasant to go walking out in Delhi wearing my increasingly dusty yellow leather shoes made in Delhi. The heat is not intolerable ... I'm definitely romanticizing it, though, because I'm leaving tonight. Reyhan insists that their house is the oldest one in the mohalla and that there is an old aunt who lives upstairs who refuses to see anyone or to be seen.

But I love this house and its paintings: one of a kitten, one of a pair of peacocks, one a portrait of Reyhan with her two sons when they were babies, plus the collection of nutcrackers that line the dining-room walls, and the heavy ancient wood furniture of the drawing room, unchanged from when I first visited at age fifteen. 11:34 AM

It seems you've had a much better time in Delhi, alhamdulillah. 11:40 AM

Delhi has been an oasis for me – it's a singular feeling. This is entirely due to Reyhan and her generosity and her (now-departed) parents' historic closeness with my grandparents. 11:44 AM

PART FOUR

As If to Filibuster
the Passing of Seasons

2018-09-01

Salam from Toronto. I had an eerily silent cab ride up Yonge Street at about 6:30 this morning. All is well at the moment. 7:52 AM

Walaykum assalām from Srinagar, from ground zero of yet another wedding, another performed, rehearsed, and fully monetized exchange of love. I wish I could garner enough emotional detachment to be able to do an ethnography of meanings at Kashmiri weddings. 9:40 PM

On second thought, maybe not. 9:44 PM

2018-09-02

Today I finished a short piece of writing about the day of my arrival in Srinagar. I feel deeply thankful to have the experience to remember and write about, because otherwise I would find it crushing to be back here in overdeveloped Toronto. This many skyscrapers looming over humanity is fucking ridiculous. 2:53 PM

2018-09-04

Are you still in overdeveloped Toronto? 5:22 PM

Yes. 7:58 AM

The cicadas have become terribly insistent. 5:33 PM

It's almost as if their shrill insistence has turned the paddy yellow overnight. 5:33 PM

I am on my way back from work. 5:33 PM

The humidity is gone, and there's a shred of the heat on the first two hours of the afternoon. 5:34 PM

For all other purposes, it's fall. 5:34 PM

It's achingly beautiful. 5:34 PM

I told Nazli Auntie about our exchange of messages and impressions of Eid and I quoted your line, "The last remaining Muslim cell in my body has now died," at which she simultaneously laughed and shuddered in sympathy. 8:34 AM

The cicada, dear Rahat.

Audio recording of cicadas chirping. 9:51 PM

I am obsessed with the cicadas this fall. Or maybe they're obsessed with me. They're like a phantom train. 9:52 PM

Thank you for this. 🖤 6:21 PM

Dear Sumayya, the original purpose, the ongoingness of our shared work, comes back to me. It comes back to me on this Canadian airplane of greys and blues. I hear your mother's voice, singing, on the open black water of Dal Lake, her homage to the rising full moon. How she waited until the right song came to her, and perhaps until the draw of the oars guiding the shikara settled into a steady rhythm. The ease, the geniality, the sweetness I didn't expect, of the oarsman and his assistant whose first stop after pushing off from the Hazratbal ghat was – this makes me laugh out loud, in delight, remembering – for tea. A tray of cups and a thermos and – were there pastries? – passed across the narrow prow, over the upholstered seat back.

The shikara is a conveyance to give the passenger assurance that the world can be made for pleasure. How old this knowledge is in my body, in my cellular memory – even as you sat upright in the stern, fighting off a worsening migraine – this knowledge of being born, if not in Kashmir then to it; to be in it; to clamber on one's childish knees into a shikara to row or be rowed about, on the lake ringed with the street lamps my grandfather made – for me, at least as much as he made them for everyone.

On this journey to Kashmir I was able to put aside the
quarrel about the sum and weight of collective loss – and
savour what we still have. I marvel – that I ever had it.

Dear Sumayya, I am back in my
apartment in Vancouver. 7:43 PM

How quiet it is. Vancouver in the rain on a Sunday in
early September. How stunningly quiet. 7:45 PM

It has been rainy and cool since I arrived. I spent two
hours this afternoon in Jericho Park with Holly Schmidt,
an artist who is currently doing a residency at the West
Point Grey Community Centre, on a walking tour of the
trees and the varied history of their growth depending on
whether they were native or cultivated. I deeply enjoyed
being in the forest. I thought of you a lot and what
you said about the smell of chinars and how when you
were here you went up to the maple trees to determine
their provenance and character by scent. 7:54 PM

Through this fall I will be contributing poetry to a project
she has created called "All the Trees."⁶ It's a remarkable
patch of land, that beachfront park, with several layers
of colonization and redefinition over time. 7:56 PM

It's the first time I've walked so purposefully and
consciously from the west all the way to the eastern
end of that place, along the footpaths in the forest
rather than along the beachfront itself. 8:03 PM

I loved your photo of the raindrops on the car
window on Residency Road. I wish I could spend
my Saturday afternoon drinking overly sugary
coffee and browsing books on Residency Road.
The rain here is a dark soggy mess – I can't make
it picturesque – but you know what it is. 9:13 AM

Dear Rahat, I have been thinking of the
times and spaces we recently shared:

[untitled poem]

It is with a heavy heart that I
Announce the timely passing
Of Summer

Dearly beloved
We who are no longer gathered
Here, now

Look forward to the transcendent trill of the cicada –
Isrāfīl of the seasons –
Until Thy kingdom come
Thy will be done.

We who are no longer
In, and of, the same city
But on two sides
Of the same barzakh
(Lā nastabghiyān)
Put our ears to the song
Of an omnipresent tree insect
With the wingspan of four oceans

"I always resent autumn
For what strikes me
As its extreme punctuality," you said,
In Shalimar, when the air was heavy
With twenty years of climate change,
The late summer fragrance of the chinar,
And "mosquitoes the size of horses,"
As one of our mothers remarked.

One of us brushed an errant hair
Out of the other's face

Without forethought, without warning,
Without closure –
An untimely tenderness passing over us like a gathering of clouds
"My heart used to be the gauge with which I'd keep time
And its mercury is now dying," I re-count
From an earlier exchange

We who have been gathered repeatedly
Into knots, bows, ties, nooses
May one day
Squeeze out of the sexagesimal rhythm
Re-naming, re-setting
Pausing
The fragmentation of leaves
Re-visiting the tyranny of autumn
As cozy-chic aesthetic

We who never again may gather
Dust to dust and ashes to ashes
Must find our way into a communal coffin
Cheeks pressed to each other's pressed to plexiglass,
Waving promises woven into time zones
Like so many goodbyes

The onus of passing is always
On Time
But the cicada holds the floor
(As if to filibuster the passing of seasons / daylight / twilight),
And I ask one of us,
"What time is your flight, again?"
And the other of us counts to twenty
Years on her fingertips
Wondering which of the cities
Withstood the test of time

3:11 PM

> I think our exchange should be published – a
> book like a cluster of thorns with some few
> fragrant petals caught in them. 10:35 AM

2018-09-23

> Whatever emotions I have around the logistics of packing and leaving, packing and leaving, are seeping into my dreams. Before waking this morning, I had a dream about a kind of castle on an isolated patch of land surrounded by water, eerie and dramatic. Light from the sky shifted the water colours on a spectrum from blue through purple to red. I kept seeing glimpses of the water through windows, or doorways that opened onto blank air, with beds of exposed, blackish seaweed below, and then when I shifted my attention indoors there were different family members who kept helping me pack and re-pack, shifting clothes and books from bags into boxes or from boxes into trunks, and constant discussions among them about the method or time of departure, of the plane or train or truck. 12:54 PM

> The water was purple, like amethysts. 12:56 PM

2018-09-30

Salam. 9:33 AM

What if I tried to translate one of your poems? 9:33 AM

I have always wanted to translate "April Is When I Most Hate Vancouver." But I had originally thought of translating to Urdu, not Kashmiri. 9:33 AM

2018-09-29

> I would LOVE that! 9:04 PM

2018-09-30

Also, "April" seems rather daunting. 😃 9:34 AM

But "Tajwid Lesson" would be much more doable. 9:34 AM

I haven't written much in Kashmiri and I am nowhere near as comfortable with literary Koshur as I am with Urdu or English. But I am going to give it a try. 9:35 AM

2018-09-29

> I know. It isn't necessary to achieve a literary level, though, so that takes the pressure off. This is just

an exercise … to teach me my missing language.
We can take it a few lines at a time. 9:06 PM

I am excited about "Tajwid," since it also deals
with gatekeepers of language. And languages
of longing and belonging. 9:38 AM

2018-10-17

Dear Sumayya, in the midst of a few intractable
miseries, I have an increasing appetite for eating pink
rose petals. Today I watched a YouTube video to learn
how to make gulkand. (I only realized recently that
I have eaten gulkand since childhood without being
aware of it, or of what it was – since we used to beg our
parents for the almost bafflingly exotic treat of sweet
paan on our rare car trips to Toronto in childhood – in
a conversation with Reyhan and my cousin about
Mughal-era sweets, which are still made at a century-old
shop in Delhi.) The video had a woman somewhere in
the south walking among her rose bushes with a bowl
under her arm, snapping blooms off their stems. What
entranced me about this scene, besides the flowers,
was the sense of dustless heat and the deep, palpable
silence of the woman's farm. At one point we heard farm
animals bleating or crowing, but then the return to the
country silence. She sifted the petals apart in her hands
and then layered them into a glass jar with sugar and
honey. It was incredibly soothing to watch. 9:07 PM

Dear Rahat, how are you? I finally finished
translating part 1 of "Tajwid Lesson"[7] last night.
With help from my mother. 10:23 AM

Koshur Translation of Part 1 of Rahat Kurd's "Tajwid Lesson"

"Zi yuth ne zyev kali (Lest the tongue stumble)
Qaeble halli (or the direction of the Qibla be missed; Kashmiri idiom
    for making a mistake of etiquette)
Te waenji aashe hinz tharr byehi" (Hope aflutter in my heart)

Wostaad aes wanaan (The teachers would say)
Zi yuhoi raviye pazi thawun (that one needs to adopt this attitude)
Timan kalamullahken fankaaran, (by those artists of the word of God)
Tajweed hyechan waalyen (those learners of tajwid)

Wostaad aes hyess diwan: (The teachers would admonish:)
Zi yuth ne galti aturr bani, (lest a mistake become a blunder)
Te lafzuk matlabei taluk-pyeth sapdi (and the meaning of the word
    become upside down)

Jabri sabqech yi dannd-dagg (The toothache* of this forced learning;
    *colloquial Kashmiri for tortuous, tedious process)
Aes mye nath tchaanan; (would instill a dread in me)
Badweni rawaeni seeth (The increase in fluency)
Os ne hargiz tasli yewaan (never satisfied me)

Patte wuot suurai Wadduha – (And then came surah Duha)
Su prezlwuni akhtaabuk suure – (The surah of the shining sun)
Te mye porr: (And I read:)
"Tche trowukh ne panein Robban, ("Your Lord has not forsaken you,)
Tchaani path-kaale khotte aasi chuon bronh-kaalei behtar" (The time to
    come will be better for you than your past")

Okhun saeb gov khosh (The Quran teacher was happy)
Mye dyutun shabash, te phyoor (Told me "well done" and turned)
Mye lari bihith (to the one sitting next to me)
Beyis bah-waershe kori kun (another twelve-year-old girl)

Aeth manz dyut myaanen nazran aalaw (That is when something called

out to my eyes)
Saheefkis doimis varqas pyeth (the other page of the Book / scripture)
Angreez khatas manz lyekhit tarjaman (the translation written in
  English)
Te yeman satran henz nazakate te halimi seeth (and the tender and
  compassionate tone of these lines)
Aaye mye aabe aech barith (filled my eyes with water)

Arbi'ik zeyr te zabar baney (The zeyr and zabar of Arabic became)
Myaanen zameeni harfan hind parr (wings to my earthbound words)
Te dyut-hokh wudaw. (and gave them flight.)

10:25 AM

I have taken a few liberties here and there. 10:25 AM

To fit idiomatic Koshur instead of literal
word-for-word translation. 10:26 AM

2018-10-31

Thank you, Sumayya. I so appreciate that you persisted
with this and that your mum helped you. 10:12 PM

I am well, in body, alhamdulillah, but I have been
struggling in soul. Being back here is hard. Though I
have seized on a couple of happy opportunities – I joined
a Persian literature in translation class at UBC (as a
guest) after meeting the instructor (who had just moved
to Vancouver in August) at an in-house concert given by
Seemi in September the week after I got back. 10:25 PM

The highlights of the class for me have been the women
poets – Jahan Malek Khatun (of Shiraz) and Makhfi
(the Mughal princess Zeb-un-Nissa). We also read
some Amir Khusro and Bidel Dehlavi. 10:29 PM

Some colleagues of Mostafa's are working on new
translations and they permitted him to use them in
class. Makhfi has a wonderfully sharp wit / intellect.
This couplet is translated by Dick Davis: 10:30 PM

I flee from knowing others so much that
Even before a mirror my eyes stay shut.[8]

My mother has been staying with me for a
few weeks – too few, really, as she is going
back to Ottawa this Sunday – 8:50 AM

I signed up for three Saturday writing sessions with
my mentor, Betsy Warland, so I have something to
get me through the month of November. 8:52 AM

Interactions with sympathetic humans are rare
and at a premium. Also, we have this pestilence of
adults glomming onto a children's holiday known as
Halloween which in Vancouver seemed to last the
entire thirty-one days of October this year. 8:53 AM

I wanna live in Paris for a year...

Dear Sumayya, my friend Marguerite just wrote to me
about Paris, where she is living for a year. She wrote
to me about walnuts, and I suddenly remembered
my failed quest for them in Srinagar. She was on the
metro, going back home from her first night out at
the cinema. And that's when she got my email.

"Just then, I felt as if the city had cracked open for me.
Like the walnuts that, in the country last month, we beat
from trees with friends, and which, at first, seemed so
dusty and ashen, but which our kids learned to ease open
with a dull knife, so was Paris to me after the movies,
on that train, passing through neighbourhoods of lights,
reading your email. I could finally taste this city!" 8:53 AM

The film she went to see was a Jean Renoir one, with
Ingrid Bergman, and you know his most famous
film is *La règle du jeu*, The Rules of the Game. So
when Marguerite writes about beating the walnuts
from the trees, a scene from the Renoir film rises
to my mind, of the beaters (the estate workers)

moving through the forest where there is going to be
a weekend hunting party, using their long sticks to
shake the foliage and rouse the birds ... 9:01 AM

(I saw that film in school and must have written a paper
about it, to have such a strong memory.) 9:03 AM

Now I feel as if I must urge you to gather a
walnut-hunting party, complete with all the grand
accoutrements for a Kashmiri picnic, even in defiance
of winter ... since everyone swore to me that the
walnuts would be ripe by November. 9:06 AM

I can see it in my mind ... 9:09 AM

Walnut beaters moving silently, stealthily
through the orchards in search of riches,
in defiance of occupying forces.

Photo of Sumayya Syed's family in the green Kashmiri hills. 9:12 AM

2018-11-21

So delightful. Khush raho aur jeete raho. 7:08 AM

2018-11-29

Dear Sumayya, how are you? Really, I am asking how are
we? How is that part of myself I left in Srinagar – 3:19 PM

2018-12-10

Salam Rahat. 9:41 PM

We are in December. That terrifying, isolating,
heart-eating month of the year. 9:42 PM

Forgive me for never getting back to you. 9:44 PM

I absorb your messages selfishly. 9:45 PM

Feeding off the affection, the connection
that I so desperately crave. 9:45 PM

Please tell me how your Persian literature
class went – or is going. 9:47 PM

I also remember you said you're doing a project with a
friend of yours who is writing about trees. 9:51 PM

2018-12-09

> Yes. I sat in on the Persian literature class
> through October – just for the poetry sessions,
> which I enjoyed immensely. 9:44 PM
>
> The women poets, Jahan Malek Khatun (a
> fourteenth-century contemporary of Hafez) and
> Makhfi (the daughter of Aurangzeb, seventeenth
> century), were the highlights for me. 9:46 PM
>
> You know that Makhfi was the main reason
> I wanted to join the class. She is one of those
> people who make you deeply wish you could
> travel back in time and meet. 9:47 PM
>
> And my tree poems! Members of the public wrote letters
> to individual trees in Jericho Park, and the artist who
> designed the project commissioned me to write poems in
> reply to a few of them, in the "voice" of the tree. 9:48 PM
>
> One letter writer said that the northern catalpa
> (with its strikingly knotty trunk and twisted
> branches) looked like a man, one to whom she
> felt safe confiding her secrets. I responded with
> "Apollo as Northern Catalpa, Instead of Daphne as
> Laurel Tree." It was a lot of fun to write. 9:49 PM
>
> Another person wrote to a giant redwood in the park,
> expressing worry about human environmental impact on
> the earth. It made me think of Birnam Wood in *Macbeth*,
> so I wrote "A Sentinel Rebels (Giant Redwood)." 9:51 PM

Apollo as Northern Catalpa, Instead of Daphne as Laurel Tree

How I resisted,
what desperation,
what denial

racked my spirit
twisted my limbs,
remains
plain to be seen.

I should have been
soft and green and easy
when I first took root:
I refused that, too.

The legend says
Apollo hunts Daphne
but suppose
Daphne, the nymph
sworn to chastity
exhausted, sick of running
to defend her freedom,
finally turns in rage
on the purblind,
egotistical god;

Suppose her father, a river god,
doesn't for once bungle matters,
like grumpy old patriarchy,
punishing the victim
when she calls for his help –

but thinks fast, looks sharp,
entreats Earth herself to arrest
his daughter's would-be rapist.

Suppose Earth smiles, flexing
unsuspected muscle,
binding the stunned god
immovably to herself:
whiplike roots
and astonishing bark
as unyielding and unlike
the supple human skin
(he now regrets coveting)
as rough-hewn armour.

Suppose, too,
as goodwill gesture,
Earth grants him
the concession
of these freakish, bewitching,
rather glorious branches.

Though I cringe
remembering
my arrogant,
sun-like entitlement,
how I pushed against fate,
shocked by the nymph's
triumphant escape; then
I'm relieved to say,
I writhed in shame
at what I'd done,
or tried to do; regretted
all the good
I might have wrought
when I could
and didn't –
a god!

But what young man isn't –
hale, swift of step
and sound of limb –
convinced he is one?

Millennia later,
we can laugh about it,
Earth and I.

Generous Earth, pulling me
from time's headlong
linear progression –
saving my life just
as she saves us all,
in richness, daily.

On sunny days fathers in jeans gloat
over first words and first steps
of their baby daughters
at play in the park

Can any of them guess
at my roots, at how the legend
went sideways;
the punishment
that wrung my divinity
of pride
but not entirely
of splendour?

Exclaiming
in pleasure and surprise –
passersby take photos

sometimes running their hands
over my wild silvered form,
sometimes moving closer,

to tell the secrets
only a god can truly hear –
with compassion,
in perfect composure.

9:51 PM

A Sentinel Rebels (Giant Redwood)

> *Who can impress the forest, bid the tree*
> *Unfix his earthbound root?*
> —Shakespeare, *Macbeth,* act 4, scene 1

Humans study my roots
for new metaphors,
connection and kinship

My limbs fuse their ideas
of geometry and distance.

Turning sunlight and time
to my family's advantage;

I gained mass
at astonishing speeds –

stoically, sedentary, forest sentinel.
To ensure our survival

I taught my children
how to absorb CO_2; how to hold it –

will you keep yours close,
or urge them to run?

Outstripping gravity's
a mere game to me now:

The shine's
gone off this job. What if I walked?

Hasn't my hour come –
isn't the season ripe
for this coast redwood to strike,
tear up the forest floor,

ring the alarm of revolt
poets & storytellers
warned you about?

9:51 PM

2018-12-11

Dear Sumayya, tonight I went to see the Guo Pei exhibit
at the Vancouver Art Gallery. It was the most dark,
dreary, rainstormy day until about 3 p.m. I was facing an
Aijaz-less evening alone. So I shook off my drowsiness
and went downtown. I thought you might enjoy these
images of dresses and shoes. Especially shoes.

Photos of sumptuous and dramatic couture dresses, jackets, and gowns,
plus elaborately beaded jewelry, crowns, tiaras, and shoes, designed by
Guo Pei on exhibit at the Vancouver Art Gallery. 10:44 PM

> I think this pair of shoes was my favourite, judging from how long I've now spent staring at them:

Photo of white-leather ankle boots covered in gold feathery wings, with each platform heel adorned with a huge red peony and crystal beads. 10:52 PM

> The gold feathery wings make me think of Hermes in Greek mythology.
>
> This is the coat that made Guo Pei world-famous:

Photo of a fur-trimmed, hand-embroidered, Yellow Empress silk cape with sixteen-foot train, made in 2012 and worn by Rihanna at the Met Gala in 2015. 10:54 PM

> I first read about Guo Pei in the film festival guide, soon after coming back in September. There was a documentary called *Yellow Is Forbidden*. 10:55 PM
>
> All about her career as a couture designer and how she draws on Manchu fashion history. 10:56 PM
>
> Then I started seeing posters around the city for this exhibition at the VAG. 10:57 PM

2018-12-12

These all feel so inspired. 12:27 PM

> I don't think my photos do the exhibit justice. Some of the fabrics & colours made me think of my cousin's wonderful series of embroidered wedding pherans and dresses, and my nieces in their carefully coordinated finery in Srinagar. And you in that satiny purple and olive pheran you designed. 10:59 PM

Okay, I am definitely going to become a couturist when I grow up! 😬 12:29 PM

I love those extravagant beaded shoes. This pair:

Close-up photo of multicoloured crystal-and-bead flowers embroidered all over white-leather peep-toe boots, on roughly twelve-inch-high, gold-studded, rectangular, open-frame, wooden platforms. 12:30 PM

> I knew you would!! 11:00 PM

Ha ha! 12:30 PM

Thank you for these, Rahat. 12:30 PM

As always, you bring me not only connection with a world I am missing out on, but most of all with yourself. 12:31 PM

> If you can imagine what it was like, after all that rain and solitude, to remember that Tuesday evenings are pay-what-you-will at the VAG, and then to go experience this dazzling fantasia ... I was elated. 11:03 PM

It must have been sublime. 12:34 PM

> There has to be a reason for me to wear a headdress like this at least once in my life:
>
> Photo of a metallic gold filigree head ornament, partially masking one side of the face, strung on either side with gold chains, crystals, and pearls. 11:04 PM

We need to invent new rituals. Have you seen the traditional Kashmiri headgear? Silver bells? 12:34 PM

> Yes, I have. 11:05 PM

Some brides have started to wear it at their extremely Indian mehendi. 12:36 PM

I am at the doctor's office, just found out that there is what the urologist called "a shower of stones" in and around my kidneys. 12:36 PM

> I am so sorry to hear about your health. 11:06 PM
>
> A shower of stones against quite the wrong target. 11:07 PM

Ha ha, but I have been reading your "Seven Stones for Jamarat." 12:37 PM

I think I need stones in my repertoire. We all do. 12:38 PM

> We do. But surely not these? 11:08 PM

My doctor told me there's a "kanni jung" going on
inside me, which, if you remember, is the weekly ritual
of stone-pelting outside Jamia Masjid. 12:39 PM

That is a remarkably poetic doctor. Kanni jung! 11:13 PM

Ha ha, yes, most Kashmiris will turn poetic on you in
the course of a mundane conversation. 12:46 PM

Maybe we need formal rituals of war against
patriarchy and capitalism that require
the wearing of couture ... 11:19 PM

It can be serious or absurd, depending on
the mood of the wearer. 11:20 PM

Yes! 12:51 PM

I want a hysterical ritual ... 12:51 PM

Something extremely anti-productive. 12:52 PM

Good. Yes. Let us make up these new
and necessary rituals. 11:22 PM

This feels very Kashmiri. 11:23 PM

Like a new way of making it possible to express
Kashmiriness in the hostile world. 11:23 PM

Ha ha, but I will rebel against every
Kashmiri ritual I can find. 12:53 PM

Or maybe co-opt them, given the paucity
of my emotional resources. 12:54 PM

I mean a reclaiming of Kashmiriness in the
name of this extreme anti-productivity you
have identified our need for. 11:24 PM

Reclaiming the artistic or craft side
of Kashmiriness. 11:25 PM

Yes! 12:55 PM

That is what taking six months to embroider a shawl means, after all. 11:26 PM

There is a long-standing narrative of Kashmiri laziness, especially in the winter months. 12:56 PM

But the most amazing chainstitching happens in December. 12:56 PM

With a kangri. And poor lighting. Or it used to. 12:56 PM

These days everything is machine embroidered. 12:57 PM

There's too much white light. 12:57 PM

I see. Has it snowed? 11:27 PM

Not yet, there is snow forecast for tonight. 12:58 PM

December is seriously weighing me down. 3:28 PM

I have had a bit of a heartbreak in the last week. 12:58 PM

Well, more a mindfuck than a heartbreak. 12:59 PM

But they both come together on one plane. 12:59 PM

Still very important to know the difference. 11:29 PM

Yes. 12:59 PM

What happened? 11:29 PM

A guy I have been very strongly drawn to for a long time, for years, reconnected. On FB. We connected extremely well. 1:00 PM

For about a week. 1:00 PM

And then suddenly he went COMPLETELY, I mean ABSOLUTELY, ape-shit crazy. 1:00 PM

I can't remember feeling that terrified since I was a girl. 1:01 PM

He's blocked and safely out of my life, but I'm left with the cleaning up, as it always falls to the woman. 1:02 PM

Yes it does ... damn it. 11:32 PM

But I think I've gotten better at it. I
am up and running. 1:02 PM

> I need to tell you I went to a kickboxing fitness
> class with a friend last week. 11:33 PM
>
> And it felt so good! 11:33 PM
>
> The punching felt so good ... 11:33 PM
>
> Like nothing else I've tried. 11:33 PM
>
> I could feel the toxins leaving my body. 11:34 PM
>
> And I slept better than I had in months. 11:34 PM

 1:04 PM

> I think punching has to be a big part of my future. 11:36 PM

Yes, the body needs its violences. 1:06 PM

Or maybe I'm just in kanni jung mood. 1:07 PM

> You need to be, obviously. 11:37 PM

I wish I could keep these stones, but the doctor said
he's planning to blast them with a laser. 1:07 PM

> Are they big enough to need blasting? 11:38 PM

Yes, the largest is seventeen millimetres. 1:09 PM

> Oh, that definitely has to go. 11:39 PM
>
> What do you think of this dress? With the crown:
>
> Photo of a white-and-silver, ankle-length, boat-necked, full-sleeved Guo
> Pei gown embroidered with sequins and crystals, with a tall, pointed,
> crystal-and-pearl-studded silver crown. 11:39 PM

It's a little more austere than the others, so I
think good for an intimidating effect, which is
one of the things we're going for. 1:10 PM

> This is my feeling. It makes me think of
> the White Witch in Narnia. 11:40 PM

> Or an ice queen. 11:40 PM

Witches and ice queens, without compromising on the bling. 1:10 PM

> I can't believe we're talking about kidney stones and bling in one breath. 11:41 PM

This conversation has been long overdue. 1:11 PM

> Couture for the occasion of stone-pelting! 11:42 PM

Yes! Seven stones for jamarat, seven stones for jumma kanni jung. A rosary of fourteen. 1:13 PM

2018-12-20

Hello Rahat. 11:17 AM

I finally had my surgery done and the weapon of moderate destruction extracted on Friday. 11:18 AM

Well, more like destroyed, Iraq-style. 11:18 AM

And as invasions do, I developed an infection and have been in and out of hospital. 11:20 AM

But in a much more stable condition today. 11:20 AM

> Sending dua for your rapid shifa and ease. 10:11 AM

2018-12-22

I am much better today, post-operation blues are evaporating in the eucalyptus and tea-tree massage oil my mother made me, and the variety of qahwas all sorts of uncles and aunties are visiting with, and the solstice sun, and a general sense of freedom from a stone.

I am convalescing at my nannihal – my late grandmother's place in downtown Srinagar where the iciness of the wind chill is broken by how close together the houses are, and how they're built in mud rather than concrete, and how much more "lived in" they are.

The morning is streaming in through the two windowpanes, on the felt namdahs my late grandmother commissioned for her last winter on earth.

Somehow, with all the small inconveniences of having to encounter the body, the post-operation bonhomie in my family has been well received – almost welcomed – mostly because it has prevented me from spending time alone in my room.

I hope your search for work has been fruitful. Sending du'ās for expansion in rizq and resources, removal of impediments, a general opening-up of the universe for you, for Aijaz, for all that brings you happiness. 11:26 AM

2018-12-21

This message reaches me as I'm about to sleep. Thankful for those two streaks of solstice light, for the vanquishing of the stone of impediment and for your rising spirits after it, for the colours of the namdah and the flavours of the qahwa.

I went out walking a short while before the sun set, and I watched the Cold Moon of the solstice rise tonight. 10:07 PM

It was like a pearl at first, misted over in the dark-blue eastern sky. 10:07 PM

By the time I came back to Cambie from Main Street, the moon had risen clear of the cloud and I stopped to look at its sharp light. There have been windstorms the last two days. 10:09 PM

The sidewalks were covered with snapped twigs and some trees on Heather Street – neighbours of mine these fourteen years – were leaning precariously and had been roped off. 10:10 PM

I think, looking at the full moon, I felt a little sick – I have been working hard at writing and was tired – with all the things that I have been striving for ... 10:13 PM

Over whose outcome I can have little to no control ...
10:13 PM

Your dua – just reading it! – your dua for me and Aijaz – is like permission to exhale deeply tonight. 10:14 PM

It's funny about the solstice. I really look forward to it. I am grateful for its meaningful simplicity – our turning point back towards the sun. Aijaz and I were both remarking on it this morning as he got ready for his last day of school. My life feels restored by its benignity to a proper, livable, human scope. 10:15 PM

Good night. Thank you for sharing the view from your convalescence with me. I feel closer to Srinagar. Also I hope you got my email update – that Shawk, who's volunteering as my editorial assistant – really loved your poems. Thank you for submitting them. 10:33 PM

2018-12-24

I went to climb the hill at Queen Elizabeth Park this morning. As soon as some cloud-filtered sunlight woke me up this morning, I decided that I wouldn't do anything else until I had done this. The milder fresh air was such a relief after the dark rain and intense cold of Saturday and Sunday. As if the solstice had been interrupted and then calmly resumed. 10:04 PM

2018-12-26

So happy the solstice opened up for you! Please soak up the light and as much warmth as is possible. I just went out for my first post-operation drive. 6:42 PM

The darkness of the night / evening is so much more generous than the darkness of "chillai kalan," the forty days starting with the solstice. 6:45 PM

The nights are less oppressive if much colder. 6:45 PM

The 40-day period of new-m winter in Kashmir. Takes place from Dec. 21st to Jan. 29th

It wasn't nearly enough light & warmth. A flat, grey Christmas day yesterday & cold & raining again today. I've come out to have coffee and be among the citizens. I have been looking at images of the peoples' protests in Khartoum on Twitter and feeling hungry for that sun. 11:57 AM

2018-12-31

Sending you some local winter-sunset pinks. Which for some reason the iPhone camera persists in reading mostly as yellows and oranges. May we find new reserves of strength and sustenance in this thing which will be called 2019.

Photo of bare winter trees against a brilliant sunset backdrop. 6:43 PM

Hope you are continuing to heal in all ways. 6:44 PM

2019-01-02

Thank you for sharing that warm palette; it is such relief from the almost cruel monotone of the chillai kalan here. 11:16 AM

Just received the first dusting of snow. 11:17 AM

Likewise grey again here; I will have to drag myself outdoors now if I want to get groceries before it rains again. What does the phrase "chillai kalan" refer to – the shortness of the days or cold temperatures? It's very striking. 10:17 AM

Dear Sumayya, as you know, nostalgia is useless. But allow me to indulge in it for a moment. My mother just sent me an image of me nearly forty years ago. Somewhere north of Pahalgam in 1979. I was nine years old, just off a horseback ride and pleased with my world. 11:10 AM

2019-01-09

Dear Rahat, what a lovely vignette from a childhood you are so intensely connected with; anyone who knows you has heard the echoes of this connection that is very much alive with you. 6:26 PM

Thank you for sharing this with me. 6:26 PM

Nostalgia helps us navigate meanings and the often-baffling congeries of the present. 6:28 PM

Kashmiri winter is divided into the three "chillas"; "chilla" refers to a forty-day period and is directly from Farsi, I think. The first chilla lasts from the solstice to January 31, the harshest part of winter, and is called chilla-e-kalan, or the main chilla. Chilla-e-khord, the middle chilla, lasts from February 1–20; it is the relatively mild cold following the biting cold of the first chilla. Chilla-bache is the ten days following February 20 and is known to have a kind of will-bite-you-in-the-ass temperament. 6:35 PM

Mothers-in-law will often warn newly inducted daughters-in-law to be prepared for chille bache, because even though it sounds benign, it will often reflect the harshness of the first part, before spring finally sets in. 6:37 PM

2019-01-10

I see. The Farsi word for forty is "chehel." 10:44 PM

This stayed with me from seeing the Chehel Sotun pavilion in Esfahan. The Pavilion of Forty Pillars. 10:45 PM

I like the peeled-off sound of "chilla." As if spoken with gritted teeth. 10:46 PM

Tonight, dear Sumayya, I finally watched the oft-postponed but long-anticipated Bhardwaj film, *Haider.* 10:47 PM

It was like going into a trance. 10:48 PM

Seeing these two things, two of the great loves or enigmas of my life, *Hamlet* and Kashmir, knitted together as if they were made for each other 10:49 PM

And the final scenes of the drama, against the backdrop of the silent woods amid the heavy snow, holding something outside the scope of *Hamlet*, something unbloodied either by revenge or occupation. This conversation about the chilla e kalan which had just preceded it. And some conviction of memory I don't have access to. My first visit to Kashmir at age two having been the longest, lasting fourteen months, spanning all the seasons. 10:59 PM

Including winter ... 10:59 PM

The enigmatic appeal of recovering that layer of loss ... 11:00 PM

That resilience, as well as the ability to enjoy the beauties of a snowy winter. 11:03 PM

This is another layer of nostalgia, but it feels more political in a way, or at least a justified form of selfishness. A simple but overwhelmingly powerful wish to run through those woods, in that snow, in the exhilaration of that air – as it must have been then. 11:04 PM

When I was there, not knowing where I was. 11:08 PM

The thought of it is like a mental vacation after a long restless monotony. 11:14 PM

2019-01-11

"The enigmatic appeal of recovering that layer of loss" ... It is uncanny (but perhaps not entirely so) that on my way to work this morning, I stopped to capture this vignette that comes close to timelessness, and I thought I'd WhatsApp it to you once I got home, and add to our perhaps singular obsession with the urban landscape and change of seasons: 2:10 PM

It's perfect. 8:29 AM

During the Christmas holidays I felt most strange on the dark rainy days. The shortest days of the year. There was no horizon visible, no palpable difference between day and night or sense of progression through the hours. My brain felt foggy. 9:03 AM

Watching the film gave me back that affirmation and clarity, which this coastal rainforest keeps dulling and blurring. 9:26 AM

At Christmas I had been looking at my photos from August, reviewing my journal notes, trying to put myself back there mentally and write something with the conviction of a beginning, middle, end. And it all felt stuck. But *Haider* has unstuck me. 9:30 AM

I like this

2019-01-20

Dear Sumayya, I had some vaguely earnest notion of going out to the park to see the lunar eclipse tonight. But as it turned out, I was able to see it rise and turn its much-anticipated red quite clearly from my own balcony.

The sight of it rising huge and silver just at about 5 p.m. tonight was splendid. But at the eclipse I had the distinct if fanciful impression that the moon was exhausted by us all. Unable to leave our orbit, so drawing a red chunni over itself. I thought of portents and mythologies. But those are the result of human imagination. Our unending need for narrative ... 10:19 PM

Including me with this text ... 10:23 PM

● 10:24 PM

chunni seems like a veil sov drape over your shoulder and my front of your body

2019-01-21

Dear Rahat, I was just thinking about this need for narrative that perhaps makes the affect more accessible, of the need for a bit of superstition, witchcraft, perhaps what is even called "magic" in the rom-com sense. Thank you for making me part of your cosmic yet personal narrative. 12:03 PM

Sending you this live cosmic update from Srinagar:

2019-01-20

Thank you for this pleasing symmetry of greys above and on the ground. 11:38 PM

> Snow arrived in the coastal rainforest yesterday, dear Sumayya. Only two days before, I had walked among a scattering of pink blossoms that had already fallen from one of the most gnarled old trees on my street. My mind likewise scatters to a hundred places at once, every day. 2:10 PM

> Dear Sumayya, do you want to read my recently revised but still highly flawed and bad-tempered long poem? It's called "Alkohol." 8:14 PM

Dear Rahat, that sounds like the perfect thing to read on this dreary morning! Please share! 10:23 AM

Alkohol

(شریف عورتیں کم لیے)

Laughing and joking to the tavern came Firaq –
Solemnity overtook him as he drained his glass.
—Firaq Ghorakhpuri

1

Distillation
forms my subject here.

Spirit extracted
from swill.

Drops dense
with value

gleaned
on the point
of evaporating.

The body
gathering itself
around a thirst
to take it all in:

Palate, pharynx,
esophagus,
bloodstream,
take their run
at the hard stuff.

Enzymes
strip molecules;
worked liver
risks fattening;
slack overtakes
heart muscle.

You see how
the sequence
appeals to me;

how its effects
lend themselves
to metaphor

when I want
a vessel to pour

insights
women bottle

to bitter vintage,
but rarely serve

when friends
assemble.

I'd like to think
it will prove potent,

this zero-proof aliksir
of my own crafting;

I'd like
the dry skull ache

nearly to blind you
before it recedes –

to school
your craving
for more.

2

The first man to dance with me
after my marriage ended
apologized again and again,
having pulled me to my feet at a party,
for being drunk.

In fact I preferred

his game good-natured shambling,
his scruffy scuffed-boot shuffling,

to the pestilence of rooftop summer small talk,
the vacant chatter of the volleyball crowd.

Really, he was gallant as Mr. Knightley;

his limbs flailed towards
some just-out-of-reach
memory of decorum

and I could give her the slip,
that wallflower pinned to my shadow
that third-wave feminist wondering

how bored the DJ must be
to resort to playing
"Sweet Child o' Mine" on Eighties Night –

Could the world have kept
this one thing intact for me

since grade eight grad, the last time –
don't tell my dad –

I'd danced with a man
I wasn't married to?

Could the point be lightness,
to twirl and filigree the air
with every sign of forgetting,
being over it, being free of it enough

to lavish a few minutes' proximity
in a republic of strangers –
no hard feelings, no harm done?

I'd have liked

to think he wanted to reach the place
where he could see I already was

that his *I'm sorry I'm so wasted right now,*
over Axl Rose's rhetorical,
Ah, ah, where do we go now?

was meant to concede the fact
alkohol had failed to take him there –

but I'd gained no elevation higher
than boredom-tinged resignation

sure-footed sobriety had brought me –
stubborn once-idealist
rage made more stubborn still –

only to this – awkwardly keeping time
with morally conflicted stadium rock;

my *no worries,* my *sure, go sleep it off,*
perfunctory, perforce;

my drunk Knightley's outstretched hand
no portent of transformation

but a full circling back *not this again*
to the darkened school gym

where two boys squared off
pulling at my elbow at age twelve,
resentful as Western Civ and Islamic Civ,
demanding I pick a side.

"Why'd you make the poster
if you weren't going to dance?"

"If you weren't going to dance,
then why'd you make the poster?"

3

In *Devdas* an extravagant carouse
winds itself around a knell of mourning.

Shook, SRK grips Jackie Shroff
by the shoulder; Madhuri rings the temple bell

in echo of Udit Narayan's
anguished tonal shift; it's she
whose most stricken;
struck again with delight
when Shroff beckons her
to the contest of the agile

her cool, self-possessed
silk-swathed dancers
against his cotton-clad phalanx
of bumbling binge drinkers

Between tavern and temple,
the dazzling call-and-response
of onomatopoeias:

the struck chalak-chalak
of the men's whisky glasses
the rung chan-a-chan
of the women's silver anklets

What's the hook that keeps me watching?
Could it be the only sexy thing

ever suspended in the air
between women and men –

the promise to meet as equals?

More dangerous than the bottle
Madhuri raises out of the men's reach,
now playful temptation, now foreboding
as the dagger eluding Macbeth's grasp

"Come, let me clutch thee" –

I wish I were quicker. I wish I'd been

born to quickness, like Madhuri,
like musicians who solve
the problem of how to measure time;
dancers who apply the science
of how to take up space –

how every taal inscribes
a technology of keeping up
with the body's innate sense,
here is what I was made for

still, as Chandramukhi,
she has no real power;
her vocation is always
to guard the line of public morals

see the jasmine-haired women
ring their anklets around its sharpened edge?

to make the work appear as weightless
as the frown that flits across her brow;

to disguise the emotional drudgery
of holding down the gender divide
as irresistibly danceable

see the men stagger all over it,
smashing glass after glass for others to sweep away?

And what rage can I summon? What divine force
will witness how I live to write the words
"women" and "men" – and no one argues

everyone knows despite centuries
of public protest, private anguish
knowing how much
of what makes us feel most alive
escapes the drag of their nets –

how the one still remains
a persistent weight
pressing down on the other.

Only Devdas has the right to drive the plot
and he does, recklessly,
having condemned himself
to drink until death

The alternative – to fight

to be with the woman he loves –

was already, always, way off the table.

4

> *I fear that on Resurrection Day*
> *the shaikh's rosary*
> *and the coat of the wine-drinking rend*
> *will be evenly matched.*
>   —Hafez e Shiraz

Other poets
are born to sound the depths
that drink closes over

inherit silences
from which
later, they'll write songs,
chaos from which
they'll carve narrative.

I'm poised
between cosmologies, considering

the pious abjuring of alkohol
as common ground claimed by men
in pursuit of devout women
they plan to leave later

then its late life embrace
alkohol as exit strategy,
as shifty late lie

It's a niche problem

I know. A narrow entry point
through which to fashion stanzas
and seek general sympathy

One reason I take comfort
in fourteenth-century Persian poetry
and its commentators
who still argue over whether
by wine Hafez meant
literal substance or ineffable spirit

And I wonder:

could rends of the taverns
of Shiraz and Lucknow

have come up with the moral calculus
that found its highest aspiration

in the dregs of a bowl of wine;
turn mischief and virtue upside down

into a club hazing ritual,
if they couldn't exclude women?

You just know
wives were not invited to join.

Imagine a rend saying
to the mother of his children

that wilfully drawing down

the curses of the respectable
on his reprobate head,
could be argued to be proof of fidelity;

incorruptible devotion
in the eyes of God,

while she scrapes burned rice
from the bottom of a pan and wonders
What kind of God buys that drivel?
Would I regret not washing this
before I chuck it at his head?

That their drunkenness
depended most on the absence
of women's companionship
remains starkly unwritten;

How else
could my rends
get away with it?

Singing praises
to the wine
thickening their senses

against a state of deprivation
the wily self-abnegators
brought upon themselves?

Not the lack of love.
Not the despair-making entrapment
of flashing eyes and tumbled tresses

luckless poets of Shiraz and Lucknow
inscribed on the pages
of my literary inheritance –

their poems recall
no sound of woman's voice
approving the cut of a collar,

or remarking on the ideal stitch
to bind a volume of poems,
their diwans contain no maps
inscribed with walks taken together
past bookshops and pastry sellers;
no journal entries

or admiring quotes in letters
remain to tell of agile variations
of her qafia or the pulse of her radif

at last Tuesday's mushaira.

Without the a priori guarantee of sex,
how their protestations of love
would bluster and fade;

drag dust back from the tavern door
across a thousand thresholds
of dull domesticity.

If they've left me
to puzzle it out this alone,
this vexed and clear-headed,

If they've left no faraway
for my imagination to fly to
in hungry hours,
no glorious arcaded past life
to colour my dream perambulations –

I can do no better
than to perfect their self-directed blame
and fulfill their hopes;

I become both the sharif aurat
of their original prescription
and the revenge of the sharif aurat

10:35 PM

I cannot stop going over this again and again
like some kind of maniac. 1:32 PM

There is so much, and everything, in here. 1:33 PM

In my head this is a conversation we're having in my
car outside your aunt's place on Eid eve. 1:34 PM

I hear you say every line with a slight shrug. 1:34 PM

Please allow me to read this over and over again. 1:35 PM

> Well. It's a relief to get it out of my head and have other
> people walk around with it in theirs. But I had the
> devilish time with form – specifically with deciding
> where to put line breaks. I kept changing them from
> short poem lines to long prose lines and back again
> over and over. I also really struggled with revising the
> second half – the last two sections especially – the
> third part, about the drunken tavern dance in *Devdas*
> still feels partially formed. I am not convinced that
> I have entirely said the necessary thing. But maybe
> what I have said will turn out to be enough. 8:49 AM

2019-02-17

> That Eid eve was one of my favourite
> nights in Srinagar. 7:56 AM

2019-02-27

> Dear Sumayya: Is this any earthly use? I
> promise I will read it tomorrow:

Link to an article by Mirza Waheed, "For Kashmir, there is only one
strategy left to try: peace," published in the *Guardian*. 10:36 PM

2019-02-28

Dear Rahat, I have been yearning to tell you how
overwhelmed war has made me, how every sight and

every sound has turned into sensory overload and I am awaiting with dread the straw that will break the camel's back. Instead of drowning out everyday fear, as most of us in Kashmir had hoped, this war and its attendant noise have only amplified every fear we had grown used to.

Mirza Waheed doesn't live here. I have also grown sick of non-resident Kashmiris "calling" for either war or peace. I don't know what to make of what he's saying. He's understandably afraid of war; I guess I should be thankful that he's calling for peace? But I am in an intransigent, ungrateful, hateful mode of existence. 12:18 PM

There are monsters in us that war, and possibly noise, brings to life. 12:19 PM

The aircraft never stop thundering. 12:20 PM

It's a terribly, terribly beautiful spring day. 12:20 PM

From my prison window I see this:

> Photo of snowy blue mountain peaks in sunlight behind a razor-wire-covered concrete wall. 12:22 PM

I work for the Occupation; I strengthen it. And the aircraft are deafening me to the sounds of the first day of spring. 12:23 PM

> I kept coming back to this photo all day today. It has been unusually bright, cold, and sunny here these last two weeks and the mountains have been unusually stark, commanding the skyline. Has there ever been an age where a woman like me could have so much privilege and feel so profoundly obstructed from inner peace and contentment because of the workings of militarized violence on the other side of the planet? 8:18 PM
>
> I feel so restless. The only thing keeping me anchored is the task of corresponding with the contributing writers for my literary project and editing their work.[9] 8:26 PM

Poetry Submission

From: Rahat Kurd
Fri., Mar. 1, 2019, 3:24 p.m.

To: Sumayya F. Syed ▼

Dear Sumayya,

I'm writing to confirm that I'd like to publish your poems "Look at the Moon and Tell Me" and "Ghazal" in the forthcoming *Puritan* supplement on work by Muslim writers. I just have a couple of notes for revisions:

For "Ghazal," I'd like you to reconsider the last sher ("Then comes solitude ..."). This third use of the phrase "Then comes" falls just a little flat to my ear / eye. Also, is "stillborn silence" redundant? I'd like the poem to end with less "silence," in fact, and just a shade more dramatic intensity. I'd like the devastation of "stillborn" to wrench more out of the reader. Possibly with the use of a takhallus?

For "Look at the Moon and Tell Me," I'd like you to consider closely whether a few line breaks could be effective for the longest lines. Give some thought to how you'd like the poem to look as a whole on the page, how the reader's eye will follow them. If you want to keep the long lines as they are, let me know your thoughts.

Thank you again for writing these poems.

Ever gratefully,

R.

Re: Poetry Submission

From: Sumayya F. Syed
Sat., Mar. 2, 2019, 2:00 a.m.

To: Rahat Kurd ▼

Dear Rahat,

Thank you for the confirmation.

Re: revisions to "Ghazal," I am thinking of incorporating your vision in two or three steps. To enhance the dramatic intensity, I would restructure "Then comes solitude …" as "Followed by solitude, carrying to term / A stillborn violence muttered in words"; where violence perhaps does greater justice to the "devastation of 'stillborn'" that you fittingly seek, while still retaining the reflexive fallout of trauma that I intended with "silence." You're right – there is redundancy in stillborn silence.

In this form, though, this shi'r seems to work better as the penultimate one instead of the maqta'. What do you think of bringing it ahead and instead moving "A flightless bird …" to end the ghazal? I have never used takhallus, but Dust seems alluring and I could consider it if you think it works in the present case.

Re: revisions to "Look at the Moon," I will be happy with line breaks of your choosing. Here are some I can think of for the longest ones:

1. Fireflies and maggots rush madly in
   and out of the blacks
   and the whites

2. It's full. The moon
   is completely full, you dolt.
   What kind of clichéd trick question is this?
   Don't you see
   how full it always is

3. But if the sky is an abyss
   And we're hurtling into it
   at the speed of darkness,

4. (The poetess
   would have thought them stars;
   But the moon was a bare thread
   When she died.)

5. "Interesting," he remarks
   he proceeds to un-empty
   my half-full glass once more
   "You know, I have heard
   Some women's moods swing
   With the moon's phases.
   Are you one of them?"

Because of the new breaks, though, I am switching around a couple of words / arrangements and punctuations in 4 and 5 above.

Please let me know how you think these work. Sorry this has turned into such a long email!

Thank you for the feedback, and for your work!

Sumayya

2019-03-06

Dear Sumayya, I hope you didn't find the Google Docs format too confining for our editorial exchange and that you feel satisfied with the result. I am really delighted by your agile thought process – to see a little of how you actually made the ghazal. And there is something so enigmatic about your mention of Suraiya Shafaq in "Look at the Moon." The rhythm in your construction of the lines "The poetess / would have thought them stars; / but the moon was a bare thread / when she died" has such a clear and satisfying echo of Ophelia for me: "I would give you some violets, but they wither'd all when my father died." Who was she? 11:23 AM

2019-03-07

Dear Rahat, Suraiya Shafaq is a Kashmiri poet whose poems and ghazals I tried to translate. I know almost nothing else about her apart from an obituary I saw for her in the papers a few years after I had first read her and become obsessed with her. Her poems would appear in *Gulala*, the Faculty of Humanities' student magazine at the University of Kashmir. I was in high school back then, but Abuji would bring home a bunch of random literary periodicals from the university, and I would look forward to getting hold of them. She was likely a graduate student. Haven't been able to find anything about her online or to otherwise verify any biographical details. But she remains, to this day, an irresistible poetic force for me.

The exchange over Google Docs has been an engaging experience. Your feedback has helped me go into the recesses of the ghazal where I had previously not ventured. Thank you for this exercise. I look forward to reading the whole issue. 4:55 PM

2019-03-11

Dear Rahat, it is 1 A.M. and I am possessed by fragments of cities I've lived in. Writing, or trying to write, this poem I am tempted to call "1st & Wind." 1:06 AM

Sharing, chiefly because I walked, perhaps even marched, with you in Vancouver a few times. But partly also because I desperately need this to be read. 1:07 AM

1st & Wind

There was no possibility of taking a walk that day.
And so I took the SkyTrain
back and forth
pummelling the city like an unoiled piston.
Distance became the shortest drawing
Between over-familiarities

Transverse sans counterpoint –
The sombre, practical geometry of avenues
Perpendicular to streets
Perpendicular to homes
Only took me so far:
from the Fraser River to the waterfront –
Foremost frontier –
First on the wind,
Then, after I had watched *Wadjda* for the fifth time,
On two wheels,
Spokes, gears, the Achilles tendon,
the power of the gastrocnemius muscle
And a singular desolation
Drawing circles in the sand:
Circles I tried feverishly to commit to memory
With the hope, the dread, the presentiment
To burn into the thin membranes of my dream
The possibility of ever taking a walk.
Everything in Vancouver
was either sky-this or Pacific-that
Planes parallel to a subterranean life
that came crawling out of the woodwork
between rains.
And so I fled.
Or chased
(whichever came sooner)
A congeries of mixed-use neighbourhoods
I tried to hold the city together
at the centre
To keep it
From scattering into the ocean;
Tried to contain, specifically, the following:
"Street Art"
"Poetry in Transit"
"Community"
"Truth & Reconciliation"
"Most Livable"
"Dale Chihuly"

But fragments of stolen land,
That depository of memory
Unanchored from smells
Drifted apart on waves of real estate
the homeless a euphemism for the Homeless
the un-homed, the dis-placed, the dis-tanced, the dis-
Possessed.

"See they not that we shrink the land
(away from them), straining it
from its borders?"
The multi-verse
(many-mouthed sonnet)
expanding to infinity
parallel lines in imperfect metre
meet at every street corner.
That is the great thing about the grid system, you see,
you don't need to remember; just navigate.
Urban design
for the easily lost.
If you try to re-member a city like that,

there is no possibility of taking a walk.[10]

1:08 AM

Much love. 🖤 1:09 AM

2019-03-10

Much appreciation for this gift. 12:58 PM

Can I ask about the meaning that
inspires the title? 12:59 PM

I recognized the first line instantly. 🙂 Love it. 12:59 PM

I love the practice of literary allusion. 1:00 PM

It's startling and so right to get this poem
from you while I'm sitting here, on the very
same grid, in this sharp sunlight. 1:01 PM

I laughed out loud at "Dale Chihuly." 😆 1:41 PM

I hope that writing & sending me this have released you into a restorative sleep. 1:48 PM

Thank you for reading this, Rahat. It felt almost as if the ghost of Vancouver was exorcised. 😄😄 I wanted to call it "1st & Wind" to index the nomenclature of intersections in a city of grids.

I knew you'd like the *Jane Eyre* reference. I sometimes feel as if you and I are each other's embodied surrogates in the cities where we've left parts of ourselves. Your experience of Vancouver is embodied, and so is mine of Srinigar. To some extent on each other's behalf? 1:18 AM

I have felt more immured here this winter than ever before, because of the sharper contrast after being with family and friends in Kashmir and Delhi. I can't go through another winter of normalizing my own alienation and making it comfortable for others. 7:40 AM

I'm writing this message in the early morning with Aijaz playing heavy metal music from his phone as he gets ready for school. The nice part was hearing him sing along to a Slipknot chorus (in his newly deep voice 😊 – haven't heard him sing in a while, though I know he does in music class). 7:42 AM

2019-03-15

Dear Sumayya, this evening Aijaz performed a live DJ set as the opener for a musical lineup with his classmates at a downtown Vancouver coffee shop. The class had planned it with their teacher for weeks / months. This meant that I could not attend any of the vigils or solemn and sorrowful gatherings being rolled out across the city.[11] 11:04 PM

I think it was a moment of grace and mercy
that instead I got to watch my son and his peers
perform live music for two hours. 11:05 PM

But the really great thing was this: Aijaz also performed
on drums for the very last song of the night – an acoustic
version of none other than "Sweet Child o' Mine" – with
two of his friends on guitars, and a girl who sang the lead.

Last year Aijaz had said that this girl was Muslim
(when Ramadan started and I asked if any other kids
in his class were fasting, since he was determined
to do so himself). Her identity wouldn't matter
under ordinary circumstances, but there was
something marvellous about watching a Muslim girl
singing *that* song, today – with my son on drums.
Something fierce and hopeful and true. 11:10 PM

2019-03-20

The faraway for your imagination to fly to in
hungry hours, the glorious arcaded future to colour
your dream perambulations. 😊 8:51 PM

May God grant both you and Aijaz beautiful
futures and beautiful spaces. 8:52 PM

Here's the vignette of a cacophony I captured at Dargah
yesterday evening, a million sparrows remembering God:

Video of hundreds of chattering birds in tree branches. 8:54 PM

Dear Sumayya, once again we have coinciding reveries.
You must have gone to Dargah on your Tuesday evening.
On arriving home for my Tuesday evening, I propped
up the phone on the dining table and played the video
of your mother singing on Dal Lake just to remind
myself of the sound and mood of that night. 12:41 PM

Thank you for restoring those lines of
mine to the future instead of letting them
remain absorbed in the past. 12:45 PM

2019-03-29

> Dear Sumayya, this poem by Anne Carson is published in the latest *London Review of Books* & since I couldn't hand it to you over the dining table after I read it, I am sharing it via a few sideways photos.[12] 5:37 PM

> I have just found out that "Alkohol" is one of seven finalists for the *Malahat Review* Long Poem Prize. The news was announced on Twitter yesterday. 5:37 PM

> I should have said the news was Twittered in words. 😂 5:40 PM

2019-03-30

I am so happy about "Alkohol"! Alhamdulillah. 10:19 AM

Thank you for sharing the Anne Carson poem. Toxic gender as performed in, and normalized by, art ... Norma Jeane the woman (and not the performer) performing as the male novelist – the perpetrator. 10:20 AM

I hear an echo of the final stanza of "Alkohol." 10:20 AM

The erasure of women as subjects in classical Urdu poetry ... 10:21 PM

But as performers in popular art. 10:21 PM

2019-03-29

> Yes. Anne Carson is a poet I have felt an affinity with at many different junctures. 10:41 PM

> Just the fact that the *LRB* is now running her work on a regular basis is telling. 10:42 PM

> There were years and years of only male poets' work being run in there. 10:43 PM

> Dear Sumayya, what are we going to do
> about the word "aurat"? [13] Sleep-deprived
> on Coast Salish Territory, R. 9:52 PM

cute lol

Dear Sleep-deprived, might I suggest that we emancipate
"aurat" from its etymology by first disowning the terminal ة ...

I love how the book you kindly copied for
me, *Hum Gunahgaar Aurtein*, subverts the
word – perhaps both derisively used words. [14]

Every other aurat, but especially the shareef
aurat, needs reclaiming from that which must be
concealed by being uttered loudly, flamboyantly,
insolently. In titles and headlines.

Over-awake from the river Sindh. 4:07 PM

> Dear Sumayya, despite evidence of the rising global chaos
> & my failing seven-year-old laptop, I am hugely enjoying
> a show on Netflix called *Santa Clarita Diet*. Tonight I
> had to force myself not to watch all the new season three
> episodes in one sitting. Drew Barrymore plays a married
> California mum who turns into a zombie, after which she
> finds that she has to eat humans to survive. The dialogue
> is exceptionally funny and politically devious. It's even
> more of a joy to see her attack and eat a misogynist than
> it is to see her eat nazis. I want to write to the showrunner
> to ask them to write a Muslim woman zombie character
> who eats every ideologue who legislates women's clothing.
>
> You may guess that I have been learning to
> confront my suppressed anger issues. 12:53 AM

Dear Sumayya, I have been thinking about your grandmother and her tenacity for Persian poetry. I read about the seventeenth-century poet Gani Kashmiri recently (for the first time ever). I was able to download a PDF of his entire dīvān off the U.S. library archives online. Which transaction itself forms a kind of poem – I read that Gani Kashmiri is said to have influenced Mir Taqi Mir, Ghalib, and others. These small facets of history make their way to me at random.

You must be facing occupier election onslaught these days. Let me know if there's anything that might aid your survival that I can do or send in support. Reading about Gani Kashmiri I loved the apocryphal story that an Iranian poet named Mirza Ali Saeb heard one of his couplets and decided to travel to Srinagar to meet him to ask the meaning of the one Kashmiri word in the verse … Having the dīvān is a spur for me to continue studying Persian so I can read it properly. I can't wait until I have cleared several commitments these next few weeks so I can go back to reading & studying. 11:58 AM

Dear Sumayya, how do you feel when you write poems? Revising "Alkohol" was strangely draining this winter. I could only work on it for short bursts at a time. I have been stringing together the pieces that were left out and they are starting to make sense. I am hoping to send you the new draft by Sunday.

I hope you are well. Please write when you can. I have climate crisis dreams and last night I was wearing a hooded rain cape in the 1950s style and I swam up the flooded steps of the library. There were traumatized fish around me. I wanted to help save them, to see them swim away. 8:49 AM

Dear Rahat, I am waiting to read "Alkohol" with revisions. How strange that you find it has drained you; after all, with distillation and essence being the subject, the spirit will find a way to be consumed.

I am unwell, I think. There is only so much one can take of living in Kashmir. I am stuck in a low-paying, meaningless job with a toxic work environment, and I miss being in a Sociology Department – something I have taken for granted ever since I started undergrad. I had never imagined a life outside of the Sociology Department. But here I am – drafting letters of "caution" to faculty members asking them to not give out statements opposing the Indian occupation of Kashmir.

I desperately want to get back to grad school. But for now, there seems to be no way.

Your dreams are always so vivid and on the dystopian spectrum. Did you feel like Noah among the fish and on the steps of the library?

The story of my library has taken a strange turn. F. decided to take my books to Pakistan, where he handed them over to a cousin of mine who is studying there. And with recent tensions, border authorities are not letting books through, especially not "Islamic" books, and my cousin refuses to lug ninety kilograms of that up to the border only to have it returned – or worse – confiscated. It is a nightmare situation. If I never see my books again, I don't know what kind of life I will be living. Please make du'ā for their safe return to me. Until I get them back, as we say in Koshur, I'll be carrying my heart in the palm of my hand. 9:08 PM

I felt only the grim necessity of survival. (And determination to get in the library, which didn't come about in the dream, but seems more significant on recollection, and in this conversation.) I felt anguish for the fish; I wanted to keep them alive, to do whatever I could to keep the earth inhabitable. I didn't want to feel helpless. 11:41 AM

I keep thinking about what you wrote. About how you would like to resume your graduate work and also about what your current job requires you to do. How it is forcing you to bend language ... 1:44 PM

To divorce language from meaning. 1:45 PM

Dear Sumayya, my mother has returned to Ottawa. I have made the changes & sent you the revised "Alkohol" and look forward to your thoughts. I've decided on keeping the title. 12:31 PM

Revised "Alkohol" 2019

From: Rahat Kurd
Sun., May 19, 2019, 12:28 PM

To: Sumayya F. Syed ▼

Dear Sumayya,

Enclosed. I think I am possibly finally at peace with the line breaks in this version.

Does the interjection of the line at the end of section one (about Western Civ and Islamic Civ) read seamlessly? Or is it jarring? And would you please review the third section especially, as that was not really complete before. Let me know what you think of the way I have interrupted the end piece about Devdas with my own parenthetical reflection. Is it effective in poetic (aesthetic) terms?

I want the whole to be a satisfying read (like a long cool drink, something neither of the east or the west).

With much love and appreciation. With prayers for our liberation and triumph in this lifetime.

Re: Revised "Alkohol" 2019

From: Sumayya F. Syed

Sun., May 26, 2019, 8:55 a.m.

To: Rahat Kurd ▼

Dear Rahat, Please forgive me for the delayed response. I am grateful for the opportunity to have read "Alkohol" while it is being distilled, to have in some way been part of its making. Thank you.

The interjection of Western Civ and Islamic Civ at the end of section one is somewhat surprising – but it reads well / gels with the dialectic at play in the preceding and following few lines. I see it as complimenting / reinforcing the contrapuntal axis of the entire poem. Although I would like to hear more about it towards the end of the poem – concluding, perhaps, with a drink reminiscent neither of the east nor of the west, or of both, distilled.

I think the parenthetical reflection of section three thematically echoes the milder drunk dance of section one. Perhaps the echo could be made a little more explicit? I am not sure how. That is one way in which I see the aesthetic sensibility of the little aside may be enhanced. Just a little more melding into the vintage spirits, the "scuffed-boot shuffling" with the first man after the end of marriage.

With love and dreams of inebriation, from the very bowels of patriarchy and extreme sobriety.

Re: Revised "Alkohol" 2019

From: Rahat Kurd
Sunday, May 26, 2019 at 8:28 PM

To: Sumayya F. Syed

Dear Sumayya,

Thank you for your acuity. These comments are very helpful. I will reread section three to listen for echoes of the earlier drunk dance and consider how the evoked tension of "east / west" is served through the last two segments …

2019-06-03

> Dear Sumayya, I'm in a state approaching giddiness, just from feeling well again after catching a bad head cold that forced me to sleep away most of Saturday and Sunday. Being able to walk and think and move and feel alert and to take part in the world around me without fever, aches, and pains is a profound relief. I was well enough today for a friend to drive me to get a stack of my books from my publisher and then later this evening I read "Alkohol," having been invited as a guest reader by a friend who had a book launch party, which was at a bar called The Boxcar and was literally the shape of a narrow 3-D rectangle. It was too loud and hectic for poetry. Especially for four different poets. But we moved outside to the back alley, where we could sit on picnic tables painted in a pastel mint shade. This evening I met several poets and writers from Ontario. Although there are a mad number of literary events this week in connection to Congress at UBC, there was still a large and lively crowd attending the Boxcar reading. 10:26 PM

I am not sure how "Alkohol" landed – either with me or with the crowd – a few people did express appreciation – but it was surprisingly easy to read despite its length. I didn't cough or sneeze or even sniffle once. 10:57 PM

The bare bones bar scene has always struck me as punitive. How do people not want hot chai at every poetry reading?

Last night, as the pain finally started to clear from my head, the men who live downstairs began singing on the patio, mostly in Spanish but also once in Arabic. I would have been so tempted to ask if I could crash their party, because the singing was so delightful and utterly removed from the everyday – if I had not been laid flat. They sang for a few hours, off and on, with all their guests laughing and sounding as if they clearly know what life or at least a weekend is for –

I wish I could enjoy these moments more. I seem to observe and experience life at a remove these days. You know how it can be just oppressively beautiful here. I feel keenly how I should enjoy it for the sake of those who cannot be in this place, yet the sense of unbelonging almost never leaves me.

Also, part of me holds onto some idea that the crust of wealth and colonial power covers up a potential power hidden in this place.

I haven't wished you Eid mubarak. I don't know if you derived any solace from either Ramadan or Eid, neither of which I felt even remotely connected to this spring. But I hope you're well and will write when you can. My giddiness about being well on Monday has transformed into an awful, racking cough. Aijaz and I have nearly ˙˙˙ᵗᶜʰing basso profundo voices from the same affliction.

quite content to skip what passes for Basic Eid l in Vancouver. But today Aijaz and I festively ˙ed pizza from a place across the street which

I have discovered makes its own lamb sausage. I must make qahwa tomorrow morning. 11:00 PM

2019-06-05

Photo of me reading "Alkohol" off my phone. 11:23 PM

2019-06-23

Dear Rahat. 11:27 AM

2019-06-25

Your poems will be published soon. 4:00 PM

[two poems by Sumayya Syed]

Look at the Moon

"Look at the moon and tell me what you see:
Is the moon half-empty or half-full?"
I do not want to sound crazy.
So I tiptoe around the cold metal of the question;
I make aerial rounds of the abyss
The pilot who knows her plane is about to crash
Fireflies and maggots rush madly in
and out of the blacks
and the whites
The story is stalled, a study in suspended anxiety:
It's full. The moon
is completely full, you dolt.
What kind of clichéd trick question is this?
Don't you see how full it always is?
But if the sky is an abyss
and we're hurtling into it
at the speed of darkness,
The moon is a genuine question
The moon is a beckoning sense of loss
A presence that stands in for every absence
A line of verse from a lifetime ago
(Suraiya Shafaq, *circa* 1999)
sprawls like a desert in the night sky
(The poetess
would have thought them stars;
But the moon was a bare thread
when she died.)
"Interesting," he remarks
he proceeds to un-empty
my half-full glass once more
"You know, I have heard
some women's moods swing
with the moon's phases;
are you one of them?"
There is no tiptoeing past lunacy, though.

And my time is running out
Before the bell jar half fills itself with stars,
At the stroke of midlife
Before the fireflies are switched off,
And my phone battery dies on me
I must categorically enter the black
And leave the white
So here I am, mid-sentence,
emptying a full glass of red wine
Over his head.
Behind me, the crescent
emerges, revolver still held to my head,
saying, "Good answer."

Ghazal

Tonight the cypress has a prisoner, caught like a bird in words
Erring on the side of wilderness, nestled unstirred in words
First comes love, then nausea, two thirds
of a season of belonging, numb-ered in words
On the margin of error, scrawled in twigs
A bonfire of errors, overheard in words
Then comes divorce, a harvest of grief
Womanhood is reaped outward, inwards
His disclaimer that love cannot be undone
Unravelling the history of desire, misheard in words
Nostalgia comes next: in re-membered
remnants of letters, love's absurd in words
Eclipsed by solitude, carrying to term
A stillborn violence muttered in words
A whisper soaring on wings of ash
Quickened as rumour, Freedom's Twittered in words[15]

Dear Rahat, how many times I've written "Dear Rahat" and been paralyzed by the scale of things I would like to share. I have slunk into a very, very dark place. I see and hear everything, perhaps too much, and am unable to utter a word.

I so desperately want to leave Kashmir.

Thank you for your work on the Muslim writing issue of the *Puritan*. It has given me so much relief to read all of these variously placed voices, curated by you. I feel honoured to be among them and hope some of my words resonate.

I pray so fervently for my Azadi. I am sorry, Rahat, for not responding to your very thoughtful and steady dispatches. Even though they sustain me and help me maintain a connection with life outside of this punishing cultural prison of urban, middle-class Kashmiri life, I often read our conversations, and I go over things you said that help me imagine a light outside of my corrupted heart and mental life. The past couple of days I have been especially sentimental, perhaps maudlin, and I yearn for something to take this weepy mess to its logical conclusion. Please remember me in du'ās when you can. And forgive me for the absences. This time last year, you were almost here. Remembering you with love and gratefulness, Sumayya. 2:29 PM

Dear Sumayya, I hope that writing this by hand gave you some relief. I wish you could be here as I start to plan a literary party to celebrate the launch of the *Puritan* Muslim Writing issue. It is being sponsored by the department at SFU called the Centre for Comparative Muslim Studies, or CCMS. It's hard to accept that I am more or less remaining in Vancouver for the summer. I want to try to keep the celebration simple and understated somehow.

I will be meeting with a poetry editor at Talonbooks in a couple of weeks. If it is all right with you, I would like to tell her about our poetry exchange. 2:12 PM

2019-07-02

You're right, it does come more organically and I find greater therapeutic release in writing by hand. I am happy with the prospect of our extended conversation become part of the community / communities we're oriented to. Please let me know how it goes. 11:45 AM

If at all possible, I would like to be present at the launch via Skype. 11:51 PM

2019-07-05

No rain as I walked out at midday today, but all the ground and foliage wet with it. I tell myself I would be deeply satisfied if it was like this every day, cool and grey for eight weeks straight, I would be content and not complain. 12:51 PM

2019-07-13

A gorgeous arrangement. 10:40 PM

What book is the top left? 10:42 PM

Top left is a collection called *Yūsuf and the Lotus Flower* by a poet in Toronto named Doyali Islam. 10:16 AM

It was her first book. An original, thoughtfully done conceptual work. 10:18 AM

2019-07-17

Dear Sumayya, shall we aim to talk this Saturday? I could call you if you will tell me an opportune time. 7:31 PM

2019-07-22

Dear Sumayya, I hope you got enough rest after our phone call. I had such a sense of feeling close to Kashmir for the rest of the day. I pray that inshallah you will get the holiday time you've asked for in September. 5:41 PM

I looked up the book of Kashmiri poetry translated by Neerja Mattoo. It isn't available yet, but I found this interview with her on *Scroll*:

Link to an interview with educator, editor, and literary translator Neerja Mattoo. 5:41 PM

2019-07-28

#me

I'm wondering if you had a chance to read my essay for the *Puritan*. I was reflecting how often in the past I've had to confine my writing to small spaces. I am afraid I will lose my ability to write in real depth at length – as certain topics demand. 1:11 PM

I have to aim high with this next book. I feel as if I must put on combat boots and conquer the body of Time. That substance which has kept escaping from me and pulling the ground from under me. 11:11 PM

| Posted today by Annick MacAskill. 1:49 PM

| I arrived in Srinagar one year ago today. 10:10 AM

PART FIVE

Premonition
Dread
Siege
Dispossession
Solidarity
Defiance

Dear Rahat, there's terror and dread in the air. 6:53 AM

Aijaz and I are in San Francisco tonight. There is news of "moderated" one-minute phone calls for Kashmiri families to contact one another. Mothers telling their sons not to come home for Eid. It's infuriating, dear Sumayya. 11:26 PM

I was with some Kashmiri friends in California this week, during the time you have been under shutdown & siege & I am trying to piece it together now. My phone was off, but my friend Najeeba had got the news of the defeat of article 35A from their families on the night of the fourth and told me the next morning. 3:13 PM

I was remembering how we texted each other during that dispirited day of Eid last year. This Eid ul Adha morning, I think again of Hajar, of the urgent need for a total overturn of established power. 3:38 PM

I am thinking of how those who have sought most strongly and violently to control how religion is performed and maintained are most guilty of vandalizing and despoiling even its outward appearances. Finally, they have succeeded in emptying religion of all meaning. 3:47 PM

I have never, in thirty years, seen so much mainstream coverage of Kashmir. Every news outlet seems reduced to a level field in access to footage & first-hand stories. 3:48 PM

That is, lack of access. 11:52 PM

Dear Sumayya, I'm praying for your safety and strength through this hell. During the last few days, I felt increasingly restless and unwilling to be alone until yesterday, when I sat down and booked a flight to Ottawa and then called my mother to tell her I'm coming. It's Saturday morning now, and I am waiting to board the flight. 8:41 AM

I hope to hear some news from you soon. Somehow. I have been venting my helplessness by tweeting about Kashmiri poetry. Even on that topic, the haters come crawling. Months ago I was invited to read poetry at a fundraiser for the legal defence of Saudi women's rights activist Loujain al Hathloul, who is in prison. It took place on August 14. After reading a few pieces from "Seven Stones" – a relished opportunity to hurl my invective at the House of Saud – I read your "Ghazal." The final shi'r resounded in that hall with even greater significance. 8:57 AM

2019-08-18

I'd forgotten that the room I sleep in when I come to my mother's house has the best view of summer moonrises … 9:25 PM

2019-08-23

I go from exasperated to really alarmed (as this morning when I see the report of close to two thousand people arrested without warrant or charge) when I read the news. The *New York Times* reporter annoys me to no end; he's so palpably a white man breathlessly discovering Kashmir. 5:20 AM

HANDWRITTEN LETTER, RECEIVED SIX DAYS LATER
2019-08-22

Dear Rahat, salam from the country without a post office. My brother is travelling to Delhi and will have internet access while there. I am giving him a picture of this letter so he can send it on your WhatsApp number. We are under unprecedented army cover and communication blockade.

This is unprecedented even by Kashmiri standards. I don't know what news you have of Kashmir – we have no news. There is absolutely no way of hearing from anyone. This is watertight. I will likely not be able to travel to KL as I had planned to – the internet blockade has meant that I am unable to apply for a visa. The abrupt beginning of fall and the bleeding edge of summer are extremely beautiful. I keep thinking back to last year when we shared this city, except it is deadly quiet this year. I also keep remembering Darwish's "Cities are smells." Today Srinagar is the smell of witch hazel. A couple of years ago – or was that last year? – during the siege of Aleppo, the internet saw a graffiti saying (in Arabic), "To the one who shared with me the siege" on the wall of a bombed-out camp or shelter. I am sure you must have come across it. The poignancy and heartbreak of the love story within that line never stop haunting me. All walls and houses in Srinagar are intact. So the "missed connection" of shared siege is neither entirely missed, nor a complete connection. We have "last messages sent" and "seen" and blue ticks where bandages might later go, along the fault lines of potential heartbreak. I have, however, managed to catch up on my backlog of readings. I hope your work is bringing you fulfillment and stability, and a year to look forward to. Please remember us in du'ā. Until we meet again, Sumayya.

2019-08-28

I've read and reread your letter, which my mother printed out as soon as I received it on my phone and shouted to everyone in the house. Your recollection of the graffiti spotted on a wall in Aleppo, "To the one who shared with me the siege." I had, just the day before, put aside Mohja's new manuscript, which is a collection of poems about the Syrian revolution – I had to take a break from reading it, as I was then in a beautiful and serene place in the woods and the content of the poem was all pain. I had felt something unnamed but definite break inside me while reading it. As if I felt some unlabelled container of hope – actually snap in half. I am writing from the car. I'm with my mother, sister, and khala

Sabiha. We're driving to Toronto from Ottawa. I am carrying your letter folded in my notebook where I have sketched out the idea for the essay about Kashmir, which I will now need to write as soon as I can. 11:04 AM

I feel as if I'm stretched between the time in Srinagar last year, your mother's voice floating calmly out over Dal in the moonlight – and Shahid's lines and "Zainab's Lament in Damascus" as the metaphor of his grief for his mother. 11:13 AM

All through the month of July, I felt the current of the energy that had carried me to Kashmir the year before, as if it was still alive. As if I could put out my hand and touch the memory current and be in Srinagar again. 11:16 AM

2019-09-03

There is news today that the army has just grabbed all of Gulmarg. And sealed it off from the public entirely. 10:28 AM

2019-09-09

I am back in Vancouver. I keep rereading your letter, feeling amazed by, and helpless in the face of, the poetry that denotes survival. 8:42 AM

2019-09-10

Salam Rahat. 10:14 PM

Salam dear sha'ir. 9:44 AM

I was holding my phone and these blue check marks appeared. 9:47 AM

It's like magic. The spell will last ten days. 10:18 PM

On the midnight of September 21, I'll turn back to Cinderella and go back to my corner. 10:19 PM

What is the source of this benevolent ten-day magic? 9:54 AM

The Malaysia trip is happening, after all. I'm in Amritsar, waiting to board my flight to KL. My brother was able to arrange the visa from Delhi. 10:24 PM

> I was hoping he would succeed – how long do you have to wait? 9:55 AM

Flight is in an hour and a half. 10:26 PM

> All right. Good. I am going to make coffee and keep you company. 9:56 AM

> How are you? I'm so happy and relieved just to hear from you. 9:56 AM

I am well, alhamdulillah. A little nervous about the prospect of visiting old haunts, but mostly relieved to be breaking the curfew for a few days. 10:27 PM

The siege has taken a toll. 10:28 PM

On everyone. 10:28 PM

I haven't heard my dad speak in four days, I think. 10:28 PM

Everyone has been more or less confined to the house. 10:46 PM

> As I had thought ... 10:25 AM

Last night I went out with my parents. 10:57 PM

> What did you talk about ? 10:31 AM

> I'm not sure if all of my earlier messages (starting early August) reached you – the blue tick marks only go back so far. These past weeks have been extraordinary – I have never lived through such a period of intense global interest in our colonized little valley. Nor have I ever seen this much of an effort to centre Kashmiri voices above the usual loud Indian and Pakistani chatter. 10:38 AM

> Yesterday there was an opinion piece by Barkha Dutt in the *Washington Post*, scolding "foreign media" for writing about Kashmir without

getting her approval first. She's probably never
had this much competition before. 10:44 AM

I saw Barkha Dutt a few weeks ago at the Srinagar
airport where she actually arrived in an armoured
vehicle with an army escort. 11:28 PM

I was tempted to ask her if she really had an ethical
ground of "impartiality" after that. 11:30 PM

But I'm tired. We're tired. The siege has sapped us. 11:30 PM

That is what makes me so angry. I keep waking
up at 5 or 6 a.m. feeling angry about this
theft of your time and energy. 11:03 AM

They stole our summer. This constantly repeating
theft of life itself, really. And the beginning
of a terribly beautiful fall. 11:34 PM

I am boarded and about to sign off. 11:47 PM

I will talk to you soon, inshallah. 11:47 PM

2019-09-11

Hope your journey to KL was easy and that the city
offers many balms and consolations. 7:44 PM

2019-09-12

The journey was very tiring; or maybe I've just grown older.
But I'm out and on my way to the university now. 11:45 AM

I find myself very nervous. 11:45 AM

I am afraid the university won't be there. 11:45 AM

What if it has disappeared? 11:45 AM

Or what if it never was there and I had
just imagined it? 11:45 AM

This is on campus: 1:54 PM

2019-09-11

If you have a chance to go to the Pasar Seni,
I wonder if the Kashmiri woollen textiles
shop will still be there. 11:03 PM

Not that that would be somewhere you would
ordinarily want to seek out ... But I remembered
my conversation with the shop owner's son there
in 2009 and alluded to it in *Cosmophilia*. In 2009 it
had been eleven years since I had been in Kashmir,
and when I saw that shop I couldn't leave. 11:05 PM

Salam Rahat. I went to Pasar Seni the other day and actually found the shop you mentioned. 12:40 AM

I am overwhelmed with the life and energy I find this place to be full of. Alhamdulillah for this beautiful break. And I just also extended my summer by ten days. Because I hear the fall has gotten pretty far back home. 12:42 AM

I am very, very happy here. 12:43 AM

I don't remember being this happy in years. 12:43 AM

This is an alternate reality. I can't seem to recall when I ever left. 12:43 AM

Maybe the whole Vancouver thing was a
figment of my imagination. 12:44 AM

Kashmir is somewhere at the back of my mind.
But at the forefront are these beautiful smells that
are suddenly so real and so close. 12:45 AM

This lush warmth. 12:45 AM

This very, very reassuring heat. 12:45 AM

My body is so happy. 12:45 AM

And I find myself planning each day around food. 12:46 AM

Chestnuts! And it isn't December. 12:47 AM

How I have missed this and yearned for this! 12:48 AM

2019-09-17

How wonderful. 10:03 AM

I feel so protective of your happiness, Sumayya – as if
it were my own. Please let me know if you feel up to
talking about this chain of letters and poems we created
and if you have any thoughts on how I can best describe
it. My meeting with Catriona, the poetry editor at
Talon, had been postponed from late July & now we are
probably going to meet in the next week or two. 4:16 PM

2019-09-19

Dear Rahat, there is too much to talk about. And with me
currently in this parallel dimension of a kind of euphoria, I
am in need of some consolidation of thoughts and a degree
of touching base with reality. For our exchange across
various zones of reality, I think of it as a stream where we
have both logged and continue to log the modalities of
our presences and absences; the stream we both know we
can't anchor in, yet it is a continuing source of coherence
and stability to us both. In our digital social & psychic
space, this is the equivalent of a periodical. 10:32 PM

The stream metaphor is perfect. My meeting is now set
for October 16, so there is no more to do. Please give

all your attention to your own heart and mind and to the things that give you sustenance. I will try to do the same – I have been struggling mightily with the same feeling of being stuck here – but it's time to turn my back on the city and disappear into my work. 8:16 AM

The good news is that I have a new machine to work on. It's the colour of a sandy beach at sunset, but it's icy cold to the touch. 8:19 AM

Still, it's pleasing to put my hands on and type. Last night I wrote a profile about the feminist scholar Sunera Thobani for an upcoming event in Surrey organized by the writer Fauzia Rafique. Now I must send my resumé to a politics / social studies publisher. 8:21 AM

2019-09-21

I just saw your "Goodbye KL" post. Ten hours ago, it says. I'm not ready to lose this link with you. 9:36 AM

2019-09-22

Dear Rahat ... 7:23 AM

I missed my flight last night ... 7:23 AM

But managed to buy a new ticket. 7:23 AM

I'm in Delhi right now, waiting to board the plane to Srinagar. 7:23 AM

May your rose-gold qalam prove to be of much barakah to you. Qalam mubarak! 7:24 AM

Your thoughts and your love have accompanied me throughout this trip. It has been magical. And it's now midnight and my pumpkin carriage is here. 7:25 AM

Thank you for the unparalleled pleasure of your company. 7:25 AM

I wish you facility and ease in your work ... 7:26 AM

And serendipity and fulfillment ... 7:28 AM

And everything you look forward to ... 7:28 AM

And your own personal azadi. 7:28 AM

An afternoon tea during the Siege: picture I took specifically for you and your mother. 8:55 AM

2019-09-27

I saw a photo from the rally for Kashmir in NYC taken by an Al Jazeera photographer today – a young woman and a young man wearing phirens, their fists raised, surrounded by supporters in Black Lives Matter T-shirts, their fists also raised; all of them with red tape (matching the bright red phiren of the young woman) over their mouths – for the communication blockade. But I can feel the image becoming timeless even while I look at it – symbolic of Kashmir's long silence under decades of occupation. 12:14 PM

2019-10-04

I've been at a mental standstill since you returned to internal exile from the world – more at a loss than usual. You are so thoroughly at home! I hope you are reading poetry slowly, daily, and dreaming in Kashmiri. I console myself with reviving such forms of resistance as the thugs who command the soldiers and cell towers could neither imagine nor prevent. 2:36 PM

Today I return, with Shahid, to Harmony 3.[16] I picture the cedar stand "with its pile of damp letters" – 2:39 PM

I stand with Shahid in the verandah as his first key opens the door. This is how I thwart the siege. 2:41 PM

I make my way back to Srinagar in these pages I've held in my hands for twenty-two years. The words could have been written today. 2:42 PM

2019-10-06

Today I stopped to eat tacos at a new place on East 5 Avenue whose hipster vibe was so high with pink hair and knitted caps the air almost hummed. I sat at the bar and drank a watermelon soda I instructed the bartender to make as unsweet as possible. The air temperature should have been fifteen degrees warmer than it was, but I drank it stoically through the slender cylinder of ice cubes as if this were Mexico.

I have a feeling for Mexico lately, though I have never been there.

It would have palm trees. 2:44 PM

2019-10-22

Today, after lashings of rain, after a federal election, after my son's recent illness, after the sun came out, after I went to Persian class – we have a new teacher, Sumayya, a man who possesses several ancient languages – Hebrew, Arabic, Greek – and who seems full of joy because of it, and whose joy seems wondrous to me, like the news of a meteorite that has been found to contain stardust that predates the solar system – 8:50 PM

Today I was homesick for Kashmir and I finally watched the film *Hamid* on my sunrise-on-the-beach-coloured laptop. 8:52 PM

Since the spring I'd been putting it off and putting it off for some reason until I think I had forgotten about it all together. 8:55 PM

Then, last week, when I came across the BBC Hindi news video that showed several elder Kashmiri women being rounded up and pushed and prodded into a police van – they had held a silent vigil in a park to protest the loss of constitutional rights & the siege – I saw the faces of two friends of my mother's, women she has known since her college day. I've met them a few times, in Delhi and Srinagar, and went into shock … 9:01 PM

And then I began looking for more information about them, finding other Kashmiris in Delhi and in the U.S. who were raising the alarm. I kept watching the video again and again, feeling terribly uncertain about what I should do or could do. 9:33 PM

And yet I also felt exhilarated to see actual video footage from the same day in Srinagar. And to see the faces and hear the voices of the auntie elders raised in defiance and anger and biting sarcasm. Just to see them! To see them taking up public space and speaking freely! I wanted to be with them. 9:35 PM

UNSENT HANDWRITTEN LETTER
2019-11-03

Dear Sumayya,

I've been rereading as much as I can of Shahid (*Country, Rooms*) to find the line that has been echoing in my head since my exchange with you – with all of Kashmir – was choked off:

The city that is leaving forever ...

The puzzle is how I could have remembered it at all,
first as I texted you in Srinagar on that day of hartal,
August 5, 2018 – exactly one year before the regime
stripped Kashmir's constitutional status – and now again
this fall, as this bullying silence presses in on me daily.

The line is from "The City of Daughters," a poem near
the end of *Country*, which I don't remember reading
more than once – or even fully – before this. At least,
I'm sure I never read it with the close and repeated
attention I've given other poems, all these years.

In the mosques of the city that is leaving
forever – suspended in lamps, with floating
wicks of oil – vessels flare, go out. The years
have come (Promise me, love, you will be there?),

... when I must spend my time on every street
in Hell. The Governor in his mansion rings
the crystal. It is refilled. The songs
in Sacredhair go out. An imperial fleet

of trucks – *No more water!* – enters the Square.
The shops are set afire.

"The City of Daughters" is rigorously structured
around the shattering first years of the military
occupation in Srinagar. The poem is densely layered
with references to other poems, starting with an
epigraph, a lyric from a Black American spiritual,
from which James Baldwin drew one of his most
widely recognized book titles: "God gave Noah the
rainbow sign / No more water, the fire next time!"

Both water and fire course through the poem's four
sections, numbered for the years 1990, 1991, 1993,
and 1994 – yet this is no linear narrative – more
a cascade of impressions; as if everything were
happening at once. As always with Shahid, I marvel
at the almost bewildering turns of the poet's mind, as

cold rains threaten to flood Kashmir: "Now who will save Noah? The Ark / is set aflame, launched." Has Shahid here made Noah a symbol of the Kashmiri people? The Ark a symbol of the valley itself?

The speaker's tone alternates from sardonic observation of the "pitiless" figure – the state-appointed governor, drinking from a crystal goblet, remaining aloof from inhabitants of the city – to an anguished accounting of destruction in the streets, as the speaker is on the point of leaving Srinagar in despair:

Share,
then, my heart – anyone! Say farewell, cut

my heart loose, row its boat without me –
for I am leaving my world forever."

Shahid then alludes, I realize, to Cavafy. It's as if he's taking courage or solace from the evidence of other poets' wrenching departures from the great and storied cities of the world – cities in themselves constituting inimitable worlds:

Say farewell, say farewell to the city
(O Sarajevo! O Srinagar!)

The Alexandria that is forever leaving.

Here, I'm unable to resist quickly going to my bilingual copy of Cavafy, to reread the original line in his poem "The God Forsakes Antony":

Like one long ready, like one unafraid,
bid farewell to the Alexandria that's leaving ...
Like one long ready, like one unafraid,
as becomes you, worthy as you were of such a city,
go over to the window with a steady step,
and listen with emotion ...
and bid farewell to the Alexandria that you're losing.

Dear Shahid,

How often hands appear – direct instruments of human will – just where your anger achieves its most crystalline form. There is something grimly satisfying about the repetitions and rhymes of the poem "Muharram in Srinagar, 1992": the way its opening line echoes the first line from "The City of Daughters," the poem it follows, but without the interrogative – there can be no question, now, just who has flown in from the plains.

"Muharram in Srinagar, 1991" also refrains an image – "a widow smashing the rivers / on her arms" – last seen in "A Dream of Glass Bangles," in the much earlier collection *The Half-Inch Himalayas*, but sharpening it here, as a kind of helplessness in the face of ruthless state power.

Death flies in, thin bureaucrat, from the plains –
A one-way passenger, again. The monsoon rains
smash their bangles, like widows, against the mountains.
Our hands disappear. He travels first class, sipping champagne.

The image of "our hands" repeats, with variations:

Our hands disappear … sipping champagne,
he goes through the morning schedule for doomsday:

"Break their hands." Will ours return with guns, or a bouquet?

Your contempt for the torture regime runs so deep, with such control – today it reverberates off the page. That hyphen, that twice breaks cham-*pagne*! Another powerful echo here, too, from the heart-swelling longing for home of "A Pastoral," of "our hands blossoming into fists / till the soldiers return the keys / And disappear."

The two consecutive poems illuminate your thought process under impossible circumstances: how to render the destruction of a world? More than giving witness, you convey, with inimitable authority, what state violence really *means*. "City of Daughters" and "Muharram in Srinagar, 1992" both transform our ability to think about militarized destruction – not to succumb to the report of its bludgeoning effects, but to ensnare them in the strong vines of personal memory. You affirm the ability to stay coolly deliberate even in anguish, to *think through* trauma, safeguarding whatever we cherished most in our world.

HANDWRITTEN JOURNAL ENTRY
2019-11-29

Seattle, WA

Dear Sumayya,

My mother just snapped a photo from 1979 and sent it to me on WhatsApp. In the photo I've got my hand linked around Nazli Auntie's arm, I'm in impossibly wide-legged jeans, I look a little overheated but full of happiness. We are in Pahalgam – that is all you need to know that I can tell you about privilege. I scheme and save every dollar I can now; I can't imagine what my future will be when I am an elderly woman. I think – I often fear I will be hungry and alone – but I went to Pahalgam as a child, several times, without a care in the world. No army jeeps that I could see: no bunkers, no concertina wire, no sniffer dogs on leashes to menace the passengers on coaches coming into the valley from Jammu through the dreadful mountain tunnel; no closed military zones; no complexity of silences around the beauty we woke up to every morning. No premonition of the murderous rage I would feel forty years later, this year, today, reading about Indian occupation soldiers menacing and leering at Kashmiri girls and women while pretending to undo their trousers. No premonition of the murderous rage I would feel writing this, today, that anything should defile the memory of Pahalgam, when I was nine and my aunt was seventeen. I must not be defeated. I will not be defeated.

Dear Shahid,

I've been scanning the sky above this coastal rainforest –
vainly, for snow. How persistent the images of ice and
snow are with you. And the outsized improbability
of another wintry image – a bag of whale bones!

Snowmen

My ancestor, a man
of Himalayan snow,
came to Kashmir from Samarkand,
carrying a bag
of whale bones:
heirlooms from sea funerals ...

This heirloom,
his skeleton under my skin, passed
from son to grandson,
generations of snowmen on my back.
They tap every year on my window,
their voices hushed to ice.

No, they won't let me out of winter,
and I've promised myself,
even if I'm the last snowman,
that I'll ride into spring
on their melting shoulders.

In these lines I can read a premonition of a haunting
to come. I scan the sky and think of Rizwan.
"Rizwan: Guardian of the Gates of Paradise." After
the unforgiving poem "I See Kashmir from New
Delhi at Midnight," whose speaker gazes steadily on
the specific pain of Kashmiri families, bereaved of
fathers and too-young sons disappeared in winter,
can the snow ever mean the same thing again?

"Rizwan, it's you, Rizwan, it's you," I cry out
as he steps closer, the sleeves of his phiren torn.
"Each night put Kashmir in your dreams," he says,

then touches me, his hands crusted with snow,
whispers, "I have been cold a long, long time."

Dear Shahid, during my childhood, I used to recoil from
the ghost stories and horror films many of my classmates
were avid for. Plugging my ears against stories of jinn –
and the occult means by which they could be contacted
and / or exorcised – according to the whispered rumours
the kids in Quran class liked to repeat, especially after
visits to their grandparents and cousins in Marrakech,
Cairo, or Lahore – I told myself that The Merciful and
Compassionate *must* have forbidden such detestable
spirits to ever bother me. I took a secret, puritan, religious
pride in claiming, for myself, an idealistic, *rational* faith.
I needed no vulgar spectacle, no miraculous visions of
heaven or hell, I promised; I would be content to live in
the everyday world, to reflect on the marvels of creation,
as the Quran itself instructed I should, based on the
evidence of my own senses – to feel moved to worship.

But when I think of how Rizwan haunted you, as if
by right – his cannot have been the kind of death to
which we were meant to resign ourselves in the name
of some rumoured will of God, but to protest – prevent
with our hands – resist. *Wa inna ilayhi raji'oon – but
not so soon* – my own ritual protest, since the day
I heard the news of your death – I'm willing to be
haunted, too. I've remained reverent in my irreverence,
Shahid. Someone could make a thoroughly memorable
horror film about the vengeful ghosts of young men
buried namelessly in cold mountain graves.

Killed at only eighteen years old, it was Rizwan
who inherited, after all, the legacy of your ancestral
"Snowmen." He is the one who rides on their
shoulders into death, instead of the hoped-for spring.
The lines coax crystalline resolve from within the
blood of my warmest yearning. *As if the cold were
my true home*, as if the memory of the woods,
asleep in winter, brought me properly to life.

Dear Shahid,

"The sky is stunned, it's become a ceiling of stone."

Four months of no contact with my beautiful ones. Eighteen years, and perhaps a few dull days, since you left us. My mind wraps itself around a bitter resolution: to refuse a humiliated silence the right to continue. That if the occupiers intend to strip the land of its orchards and cypresses, I must hold their uprightness all the more steadfastly in my mind.

Was there anything in the lines of my palms that could foretell that as my life circled towards its half-century, I would find no better way to keep malice from overwhelming the earth? Forget fate: only the lines of your poems hold any prescience. I recite them aloud to drown out the incoherence of news broadcasters obediently relaying, without question or critique, every statement issued by the state, whose favourite word is "normal."

Again I've returned to this country
where a minaret has been entombed.
Someone soaks the wicks of clay lamps
in mustard oil, each night climbs its steps
to read messages scratched on planets.
—Agha Shahid Ali, "The Country without a Post Office"

Dear Shahid,

I've been watching *Haider* again. I feel like Rebecca in the Daphne du Maurier novel, opening with a wry, reluctant admission. *Last night I dreamt I went to Manderley again.* Hers is such a simple tale compared to yours and mine, but today I'm struck by every subtle feeling the line evokes, especially wonderment. I never learned the trick of summoning lucid dreams, so here I am – streaming.

I'm streaming *Haider* so I can dream, on this first
day of the year, in this perpetually cedar-scented
time zone lag, that I'm back in Kashmir; so this
cold in my fingers can have a context; the chill in
my bones wake me to something other than how
long I've lived in coastal unbelonging. I'll bend my
distance to the purpose, Shahid, like Bhardwaj and
Peer bending Shakespeare Sharif to Kashmir's.

There have been so many Hamlets. After watching
Brent Carver perform as the prince on a field trip to
the Stratford Festival with my English class, I bought
a souvenir, a T-shirt I've often wished I still had,
screen-printed with an elegant pen-and-ink drawing
of the Dane; moody, a bit cartoonish, in black, with
a lace ruff, holding a skull. Literature worked its
way deeply into my brain like this, with an image
that convinced me – I was so pleased and proud, at
seventeen, to have arrived at such an adult sensibility – I
could sympathize with Hamlet's world-weariness.

And after that first Stratford play, after avidly watching
a string of stage and screen Hamlets, another version
came back to me in an indignant quotation. *I do not
know / Why yet I live to say, "This thing's to do"*: my
fortieth birthday was behind me, and I had still not
written the poem I'd planned to write about crossing
the Wagah border from Lahore to Amritsar one hot
August morning in 1998. I had been on a slow overland
journey to Srinagar, and the two armed-to-the-teeth
nationalisms on vehement display had somehow
reminded me of Kenneth Branagh's Hamlet, spitting in
rage over *the imminent death of twenty thousand men*
while Fortinbras's army marched past in the distance.
His acting in that scene had seemed ridiculously
overwrought, until, when I came to Wagah, despair made
me want to kick and scream and claw the earth, too.

How strange, all these years later, to see Hamlet
transformed into a son of Kashmir, by quite another

Shahid – how strange and magically *apt*. If only you
were alive to see him! As if Hamlet's true destiny was
always here; always ours – Ophelia's too, trapped
in knots of loyalty to father, lover, brother – and
their final reckonings in Himalayan snow.

2020-01-04

I bought an overseas calling card. I have been
carrying it around since the Saturday after Christmas.
I hope your account is still active. 11:59 AM

2020-02-06

Dear Sumayya, I have attempted to call you with several
false starts and failed connects. Are you no longer
using WhatsApp? I will email you. I am guessing you
only have internet access at work. I had hoped you
might have cell reception at home by now. 9:08 AM

2020-02-07

Dear Rahat, it's a foraging economy. We hunt for internet
and we gather it in VPNs and then we distribute it unequally
among us according to the favours we want in return. 3:12 PM

My internet-addicted colleague sometimes gets up from his
chair and declares he's going out for a puff of internet. 3:13 PM

And he goes to the top floor of the
administrative building at work. 3:13 PM

Which has Wi-Fi. 3:14 PM

Sorry I missed your call last night. 3:16 PM

For now I have access to WhatsApp. 3:17 PM

Through a VPN. 3:17 PM

There's a fear that VPNs may be blocked. 3:18 PM

In which case I would still be able to access my email. 3:18 PM

I hope things have been great at your end. 3:18 PM

This is along the foreshore of the lake the day before yesterday:

Photo of Dal Lake with mountains and a pink sky across the lake. 3:10 PM

I have been trying to outrun the usual predators here. I had a few weeks and then a few months of starting to believe that my pace was increasing. That I was in some kind of lead. And then during the late afternoon of January 22 I started to feel an irritation in my throat and a headache coming on. 8:09 PM

And then I missed the next four Persian classes. 8:15 PM

2020-02-20

Dear Sumayya, I've transferred our full correspondence into emails – dated and time-stamped. I'm anguished by how much of a toll the siege has taken and at the same time humbled and grateful. It may be a slim volume in the end, but I think we have created a fierce, substantial body of work. 9:23 AM

2020-04-03

Hello Rahat, thanks for this. How have you been? 12:08 PM

My Google account is out of storage or something and so the emails are docked and with the internet I have I'm not able to renew my storage. 12:58 PM

I am able to use WhatsApp and Facebook, though. 12:58 PM

Makes sense that you would run out of storage during the internet shutdown. 12:29 AM

Did you receive all my messages here? I think some might not have gotten through. 12:29 AM

The last message I have from you here is from February 6. 1:00 PM

Yes. The one I sent to you on Feb 20 didn't reach you. 12:30 AM

And I'd sent a picture of the Dal after that. 1:00 PM

Yes, on the 7. 12:31 AM

I should have kept trying to call you. 12:31 AM

But I am mentally very scattered. 12:31 AM

Could you please forward the emails to my brother's email, which I can access right away? 1:02 PM

Okay. 12:32 AM

How are you dealing with the condition? 1:02 PM

Sumayya, I'm so thankful to hear from you. 12:37 AM

In a way – with my thoughts being with Kashmir under lockdown since August – the substance of my inner life has not changed much. 12:38 AM

Or my outer life – the material conditions of it – I was already staying home quite a lot. And quite limited in the people I spent time with. 12:40 AM

But of course, things are very different with much of the city having closed down or slowed down, and with the active need to stay home and avoid people. I have had moments of real fear about how I'd possibly cope if I get sick. 12:43 AM

And this week, I found it really difficult to focus on my Persian class; I had no energy to do my writing assignment for it. 12:44 AM

I think your connection must have dropped. 12:44 AM

It keeps coming and going, but I'm here. 1:20 PM

Please tell me how the city has changed for you. 1:21 PM

As for me, this lockdown brings little novelty. 1:21 PM

> The biggest change is that I no longer need to wake up at 6 a.m. to get breakfast ready for Aijaz or to catch a 7:30 a.m. bus for Persian class at UBC three days a week. I've been staying home and close to home. 12:52 AM

And is your Persian class offered online? 1:25 PM

> Yes, we had our first class using Zoom on the 16th. 12:56 AM

> Class has been a piecemeal and disorganized experience, with the different instructors and then the schedule change this winter. I don't feel like I have methodically built up my ability to comprehend the language. I feel I'm just scrambling to write down lists of random words, with no time to absorb and practise or memorize anything. 12:56 AM

> Right at the start of the winter term, the U.S. threatened war on Iran, and then days later, the tragedy of the Ukrainian flight from Tehran, which inflicted terrible tragic losses on so many Iranian families across Canada. 1:00 AM

> I've forwarded the emails to your brother's account. I should sleep now, it's 1 a.m. – I've been staying up late like this since the early rising imperative has dropped away. But I should join the Zoom session at 9 a.m. tomorrow. 1:03 AM

Have a peaceful night, Rahat. I will go through your emails and we'll continue, inshallah. 1:36 PM

> I hope we can connect again soon, maybe Friday night for me & Saturday morning for you, if possible. Or I can try calling. 1:06 AM

> Thank you. I will try. Shab ba kheyr. 1:06 AM

Shab ba kheyr. 1:36 PM

2020-04-04

> Sumayya, were you able to read the emails
> on your brother's account? 11:19 AM

> There is nothing but a bunch of emails
> from my lawyer today. 11:19 AM

> And I would like to know what you think of the
> publication offer for our Kashmiri exchange. 11:20 AM

2020-04-05

Reading your emails feels like such an indulgence
after long months of privation. Thank you for the
abundance of grace, Rahat. The months have been
overwhelming, but also transforming – opportunities of
solitude either wrung from or forced onto an ineluctable
predicament of despair. The two mutate into each other
like shadows, with only God drawing the lines.

I went for Umrah in January – a pilgrimage I had
vowed I would never undertake. But even under the
curfew and the privation, the elements conspired, and
during December I battled this thirst to consume the
"vicinity of God." For those of us whom Faiz calls "ham
ahl-e-safa, mardood-e-haram,"[17] I felt impelled:

> aaiye haath uthayein hum bhi
> hum jinheiñ rasm-e-du'a yaad nahīñ
> ham jinheñ soz-e-mohabbat ke sivā
> koī but koī k̲h̲udā yaad nahīñ[18]

Of course, I did manage to literally become "mardood-e-
haram," being a woman in Saudi-controlled spiritual space.

At work, the staff union held a week-long strike in the
face of the imperiousness of the administration, which is
an appendage of the Indian occupation. With cunning
and coercion, the strike was quelled, and we are now
being denied wages for the entire month. I am deeply
torn about my response to this, given my fundamental

disrespect for institutional authority in general, and for the university administration in particular. Due to the COVID lockdown, we're unable to organize for now.

It's a painfully beautiful spring morning, and I am in my mother's garden, soaking up the sun. Sometimes this place reminds me of Stanley Park. But I spent way too many hours contemplating self-harm and suicide in Stanley Park, and it never reminded me of my mother's garden. So I am here now, very, very thankful to have healed and become whole.

Merajuddin, who looks after the gardens, insists that the pomegranate needed to be pruned – it is no longer blossoming this year. But my niece told him she needs the oxygen. My niece also exclaimed, during the siege last summer as we went out for a walk, "I am a beggar for roses!" 11:03 AM

2020-04-04

> I wasn't able to bring myself to leave my apartment today, as if the sun – I'm reminded of our exchange about Aharbal and me on the rocks there in 1985 – the sun on Vancouver wasn't good enough for me, and I needed to have the evidence of this sun, on this patch of Kashmir, instead. 10:53 PM

> I am floored to learn of your hours of gloom and pain in Stanley Park. 10:55 PM

> Your reference to Faiz makes your Umrah sound like a thing of wonder! I want to know more about how you became the mardood e haram –

> Your niece is brilliant – thank you for serving as her biographer, especially for that last line. 11:28 PM

> I wrote a poem about rosewater, just as the quarantine was beginning. And to my own surprise, I kept coming back to it, kept getting more involved with it, especially at night when I thought I would be sleeping.

> In the daytime, I wondered if there would be any need for poetry ever again. 11:35 PM

Rosewater in Quarantine

Slender bottle, scent immemorial. Pause
in a deepening bewilderment. Cool splash
of vanity in a stoic season, redolent
of another century's pleasures –

Remember sugar-soaked petals
cooked in strong sunlight?
Remember Persian poetry in a faraway style
Hafez of Shiraz likened amusedly
to candy crunched in parrots' beaks?

Today's quick kitchen pantry scan
predicts my prospects in plague, in siege;
whatever war's to come. You gleam

in straitened circumstance
behind a box of pasta. Little gift
of lax global trade rules, distilled in Beirut –

you might have perfumed the hands
of Mandelstam's blessed women, or Shahid's –
but at Jasmine Halal on Main Street I paid

the three-dollar sum neon-stickered to your neck,
to feel on my face the mist of imagined continuity
from August roses climbing warm Wazir Bagh brick

to pink cotton wisp, tied in ceremonial promise
to starry perforation screening a Delhi poet's
petal-strewn tomb, a deposed king's, a saint's –

my bid for survival snags on your filigree.
You're a fanciful lyric
tricked out of isolation's steady grey thrum.

11:41 PM

2020-04-07

Dear Rahat, thank you for "Rosewater." I am reading
it in continuation with "Alkohol" and in the spirit of

essences. In both, I read the "imagined continuity" with a poetic heritage: at once loss as well as burden.

Mecca was such strange territory: familiar to every nerve ending from an ancient anticipation, but almost hostile to my embodied existence as a woman. The overwhelming feeling while inside the precincts of the haram was that of harassment. I was on edge from the heavily policed architecture of a premises which my soul had trained me to expect as the ultimate space of reckless abandon. The "volunteer squad" is almost a militia, and you are constantly under threat of being asked to move, to not be there, to disappear, to get out, make way, yalla! I broke down as I felt utterly unwanted, abhorred. I was a polluting presence. I do not know how women have not burned the place down yet. I do not know how Desi Muslims continue to revere the Saudi regime as "custodians" of the two harams when they so clearly are usurpers with no moral claim to the office. Mecca was my ultimate un-mosqueing.

But in the vicinity of the Kaaba and the Tawaf during which everything melts, the Saudis disappear (God smites them), the entire geopolitical realm and the universe seemed to converge to a void in the middle of the desert where nothing else but a well of miracle water gurgled nearby and I was water. Everyone was water. You run into no one. The universe is an all-consuming fluid and you are its viscosity. The heart became almost palpable.

My disgust with the Saudi state has only deepened – but so has my desire to reclaim the sanctuary from the clutches of this evil kingdom. Inshallah. In disjointed, formal-sounding Arabic, my mother cursed out the guard at the Black Stone, telling him, يعذبكم الله.

"Damn it, has no woman / left record, in praise of hurling's righteous outrage, pelting's vicious joy?" after the fashion of your "Seventh Stone," dear Rahat, my favourite stone.

During the period since August last year, the Months, I did not write much; but I did embroider, and although the stitches aren't Kashmiri and the pattern is gaunt, I like to think I am reaching out to some part of my own heritage, since my grandfather was a needleworker of the finest class. 8:15 PM

Thank you for this – alhamdulillah for your survival of the Months; for your soul's receptivity to the Tawāf as it was meant to be received; for your inscribing on the cloth with needle and thread. 10:03 AM

It's a bright spring morning here in my alley. I need to wash my face so I can read your words again. 10:05 AM

"I do not know how women have not burned the place down yet!" 10:18 AM

Your desire to reclaim the sanctuary feeds into an idea I've been mulling over off-and-on for the last year and a half, a book of feminist incantations. 10:20 AM

It would ideally be a compilation of multiple women's voices ... calling upon the divine life force, wresting it back from the ridiculous self-appointed guardians of male supremacy. 10:25 AM

I was watching an Abida Parveen performance on Coke Studio earlier this winter ... The lyric is "Balaghal 'ula be kamalihi" ("He attained the heights through his perfection") ... 10:35 AM

And towards the end she sings "ya Muhammad" over and over again. 10:36 AM

I was thinking about the meaning of the name Muhammad and wondering whether we could understand it to convey the idea of one who is praiseworthy *because* they give thanks and praise to the Creator. 10:40 AM

Some of this is to do with my own very stripped-down, emphatically puritan Islamic education, devoid of any Sufi content. As a teenager, I was personally fired up by the idea of worshipping an ultimate, unseen, transcendent divine in splendid isolation. My favourite image from

the Seerah was that of the still-youthful Muhammad
withdrawing from the world to meditate in a cave
in the mountains ... that aloof lack of need for other
people appealed to me deeply in those days. 10:41 AM

2020-04-10

Dear Rahat, are you familiar with Al
Firdaus Ensemble? 10:59 PM

I don't think so. 11:49 AM

2020-04-11

It's a Sufi (North African) musical group
that I have grown to love over the past year,
especially their "Celtic Salawat." 12:24 AM

Link to a YouTube video performance of "Celtic Salawat" (song of peace and
blessings for the Prophet Muhammad) in a mix of Celtic and Andalusian
musical styles by the Spanish-based Al Firdaus Ensemble at the Hotel
Puerta Nazarí in Granada, Spain. 12:25 AM

I have found it especially helpful in the
Months. And now. 12:26 AM

And when you talked about the incantation,
I thought of this. 12:26 AM

I think something like this, dedicated to incantation, takes
the Coke Studio–Abida Parveen line further. 12:28 AM

With its much finer grain, I think. 12:29 AM

Without the compulsion to be edgy, which is what I found
so gross in regular Vancouver Sufi circles. 12:32 AM

2020-04-14

Thank you for the musical nourishment. I have
been at a low ebb with my divorce. Every step of
the process eats money; and then my lawyer is so
gloomy. You would think that would be my role,
not hers. It's like having an expensive, exotic pet.
Trying to please a turtle or an iguana would be more

fulfilling. I am stuck with her for the remainder of this soul-sucking ritual, however. 12:15 AM

I wrote the final exam, on Zoom along with my classmates, for Persian 201 this morning. For some hours at least, my mind was focused and my thoughts were quiet. And a little baffled, to be honest – it seems to require a huge number of words to express something that would be very simple in English – but I can't be a valid judge until I start reading more formal texts. 12:17 AM

Dear Sumayya, my last remaining thought to share with you before I shut off this phone and the lights and cover my eyes with the silk scarf my cousin gave me that summer in Srinagar – is an invocation which has been repeating in my head for some weeks – it sprang up involuntarily – since before the pandemic, with no apprehension of the pandemic. Just this: May God crush the lungs of our enemies. 12:20 AM

2020-04-17

Dear Rahat, there is a kind of gnarly dis-ease to knowing you have to deal with a lawyer – a divorce lawyer at that – during the plague. May God the Lord of love and rosewater send you ease. And indeed, may God the Lord of the corporeal crush the lungs of our enemies.

I'm glad your Persian exam is finally over. Is that the end of the course or does it have another semester? Are you keeping a journal in Persian? I was reading Jhumpa Lahiri's *In Other Words* and I'm fascinated by how the language itself became the story. If you have something you're writing in Persian, would you please share it with me? It must be thrilling to watch a language integrate into you, to watch it become you in real time.

Did I tell you that my books are now in Johor Bahru, Malaysia? After making the journey from Vancouver to Chicago and back two years ago, they were shipped to Karachi, and thence to Bahawalpur, from where I had no way to get them. After more than a year of heartache and intense du'ā, I hear seventy-five kilograms have safely arrived in Malaysia. I am hoping the final leg will be Malaysia to Kashmir when I or someone else from my family travels there. Inshallah. They include my teenage journals and books I had stolen from my grandmother and from my parents and their marginalia and mine and dried roses.

My mother has two patches of extremely fragrant peppermint in the garden. I have been putting it in everything. There are two specific nooks where it has been growing wild for the last thirty years. Anyone walking outside can smell it and sometimes we even have a little old lady or someone who was just passing by and was stopped in their tracks by the fragrance come in and knock at the door.

The house directly across from ours is empty, but the lights in the main bedroom, which faces the street, are always on. The old couple that live there had gone to visit their son in India, and now they're unable to return. I miss them. Mr. Lanker likes to listen to *Sada bahaar naghme* at 6 p.m. on All India Radio, and because the windows are always open and the breeze is wise, the songs waft their way to our living room. My father actively dislikes music, but sixties and seventies Bollywood music makes him particularly uncomfortable. He dashes out of the room, after shuttering the windows. If it weren't so funny, it would be heartbreaking. Which it still is. I miss Mr. Lanker's presence. He brings this street alive. Also, there are cherry and almond blossoms in his garden. In late May there'll be roses.

Rahat, a migraine is oncoming; I can feel it behind my eyes. I will try and see if steam inhalation helps. I will leave you with thoughts of every kind of strength! Khuda hafiz. 12:03 AM

2020-04-16

> Dear Sumayya, I am far from fluent enough to write in Persian. I can think and write in French. I absorbed its rhythms and patterns in the formative years. And I enjoy the sensation of escaping from English when I'm in Montréal and can have a full conversation

with fellow train passengers or buying stamps at a dépanneur. But in all other languages I feel I am a pauper clutching fragments. I used to think I spoke Urdu quite well until that second or third faltering week when I was last in Srinagar, and the thought of my previous confidence is embarrassing now. 6:26 PM

When I see your photos and read your descriptions of the fragrant garden, I feel as if I will be there soon – as if I'm just going to come and stay with you, and my arrival will be ordinary, unexceptional – perhaps on the same flight as Mr. Lanker, when the pandemic is over … 7:15 PM

And there is just a breath or two before occupation rushes into its vacuum. 7:20 PM

Let me plot how I might inveigle myself into that breath. 7:27 PM

2020-04-17

Intensely bored teen agreed to go for a walk with his mother today – an event worth recording. 5:47 PM

2020-04-21

I try to photograph these blooms every spring without success:

Photo of unidentified blooms. 9:13 AM

Up close they are a bright magenta but at a distance the branches look nearly purple. 9:15 AM

There are two trees like this, on Heather St., about three blocks away from my place. No one has been able to tell me what they are. 9:16 AM

Rahat, this seems to be a Judas tree. 10:39 PM

🫥 10:39 PM

> I am actually wondering if the cluster of blooms right on the trunk can have taken seed from elsewhere. 10:10 AM

I have seen a bunch of them on the campus of Kashmir University ... they seem to have a flowering trunk. 10:41 PM

> Yesterday I managed to go for one of my old pre-pandemic-style walks – sauntering without too much hindrance. It was an exceptionally beautiful afternoon / early evening. And there was a freedom in walking with no other purpose. 10:12 AM

April is when you most hate Vancouver 😊 but yes, April also is when it is exceptionally beautiful. 10:45 PM

> Indeed ... there is so much to hate. 12:09 PM

2020-04-22

> Dear Sumayya, this is one of Mohja's unpublished poems which chimes with my idea about a collection of feminist invocations. I've got her permission to share it with you.

Amulet for a Graduate Student

Pick a mantra – any word you like,
habibti – Virgen de Guadalupe,
anemone, Inanna
Say: with this word I shield

Make you a special mark
Ink it small on the doorjamb
Say, with this mark, I confound
every colonizer and whoever
spread the slander
that I'm fucking for my grades

Create codes. Say in class,
"That's noteworthy," your code
for "Fuck your misogyny"
Document everything noteworthy
Plant your elbows wide on the workshop table

Against apartheid, activists used sugar
A cup spilled disabled tank engines
Keep talking when he interrupts
That's your sugar

Surround yourself with allies
Say: I sing to the scarab power in myself
hymns like unto Inanna
until I walk away with my degree
until I am powerful enough to file a lawsuit

10:54 PM

2020-04-22

I am only beginning to really grasp how much anger
I have been taught to suppress and hold and for how
very, very long – I need a place to write this. 10:56 PM

I am also trying to keep notes every day about the
gnarly process in which I am ensnared. There is
a purpose to my anger. I need to trust myself, to
trust my anger to guide me – I have always been
very slow to anger, so I do trust its judgments; even
its curses and despair have a purpose. 11:00 PM

2020-04-24

Oh Rahat! 4:14 PM

That is such an apt poem for what we constantly need to ward
off in our circles. I wish I had had this as a graduate student
at UBC. Please give my thanks to your friend Mohja for this.

It also suddenly brought to mind something I did
actually write at the beginning of the siege. Only half
serious. But I want to share it with you. 4:15 PM

How to Cultivate Inner Peace

Summon the Demon-in-Chief
De-escalate
Over salted tea and sugared scones

First things first:
"I call dibs on poetry,
The City,
Nostalgia.
You may keep the photographs,
The dried flowers,
And all recipes involving tarragon.

Keep off the grass
In summer
Inside Jamia Masjid, Srinagar.

Don't touch the cicadas,
the seasonal raw nerves,
Or calligraphy

Take the smell of snow,
The musk-filled armpits of desire,
The unfinished jigsaw with the haunted cats.

Leave me my grandfather's embroidery
Crocuses
My collection of silk scarves."

You see, the secret to inner peace
Is an unfair deal with the devil.

Inner peace is two blocks removed
From the emptiest place imaginable; only
A gathering of non-unionized demons
Holding up the traffic.

So let me keep my earth-shattering orgasms
To help disperse the blockade;
Inner demons are notoriously resistant
To tear smoke.

> Burn sage – y'know, standard operating procedure –
> Recitation, the rosary,
> *The Communist Manifesto.*
> But also: sleep naked on midsummer nights.
> Fill your mouth with wasps.
> Burn down the fucking city.

4:50 PM

I am also reminded of Akbar Allahabadi's quatrain
that my father has always liked to recite:

> Na laisans hathyar ka hai, na zōr
> Ki Turki ke dushman se jā kar laren
> Tah-e-dil se ham kōste hain magar
> Ki Itlī kī topōñ mein keede padeñ[19]

4:52 PM

I think this is funny. 😂😂😂 4:55 PM

But also kind of recommending a unique mode of resistance
for people in situations of resource depletion. 5:01 PM

The occult is, after all, a resource we seldom
consider resorting to. 5:03 PM

Especially as women, though, we need to re-appropriate
our claim to be-witch in supra-aesthetic terms. 5:06 PM

And as women of colour inhabiting the social universe
of capitalist heteropatriarchy, to hex the system via our
access to higher orders of representation. 5:10 PM

And affect. 5:10 PM

Reading Mohja's "Amulet" and being reminded of the lines I
wrote in August last year has suddenly brought into sharper
focus your expression of the need for specialized invocations
and incantations. Your anger, our anger, is not just valid
but also life-giving and life-cherishing – crushed lungs

and seven stones and all. Thank you for the perspective, Rahat. I hope this helps us march into Ramadan with a little extra energy. Have a mubarak month. Oh also, here's a Kashmiri expression I have heard my aunts use against the male gaze: may their eyeballs explode. 🖤 5:13 PM

> Salam dear Sumayya, what an aptly timed curse! 8:54 PM
>
> Final order for divorce, signed and filed a few hours ago. 8:55 PM
>
> The First of Ramadan, April 24, 2020. 8:56 PM

2020-04-26

Salam! 10:22 AM

May this be mubarak! 10:22 AM

And a huge relief. 10:23 AM

2020-04-25

> It is. Yet I cannot fully realize it. Being alone in this aftermath; unable to hug my mother, or my friends, all of you who lightened my burden with long-distance love and support. The reality of the pandemic pours over me in a cold wave. Dear Sumayya, please inhale some deep breaths of azaadi when you sit in your mother's garden today. 10:46 AM

2020-05-03

Dear Rahat, the exhaustion that comes from being perpetually braced for "likelihood" hovering like a giant on the horizon of everything is probably the largest drain on our emotional resources as women. Sometimes I wonder, if we were a little underprepared, a little more languorous, as if we owned the spaces we occupy and had some kind of a right to other people's time and attention, what gains we could make in terms of our own poise and the possibilities of being at peace. But then this all-consuming alacrity is constantly scattering us into elements which, if we were to seize our wholeness, would strengthen the power of our presence. This shrinking of our performative selves in favour of efficiency in such a capitalistic sense of productivity gnaws at the soul as if it were an actual bone. When I'm at work, as a clerk who sits at the desktop eight hours a day, I am encouraged to take frequent twenty-second breaks away from the screen so my eyes can refocus. Somewhere in my body I feel that as a crass violation of my self.

I wish your nerves rest and repose. 3:10 PM

2020-05-05

> I was able to take better photos of the two purple-blossoming trees on Heather Street today as I set out on a longer walk:

 Photo of purple blossoming branches with a willow tree backdrop. 6:37 PM

> The trunk and branches of the second one (against the backdrop of the young willow) have a very dark, withered, slightly bewitched aspect. 6:39 PM

> I am not sure why I have always become so obsessed with them every spring – perhaps they don't belong here, like me. 6:40 PM

> Perhaps the flat concrete & condo surroundings injure their dignity as much as mine. 6:42 PM

> It is both stunning and entirely mundane that the commerce of condo construction and the buying and selling of property have not, do not, will never stop for pandemic. 6:46 PM

Dear Sumayya, the U.S. Pulitzer Prize for Poetry has been awarded to Jericho Brown, a poet I had first come across some time ago on Twitter. I am very struck by the confluence between the news of ongoing killings by the state forces of boys in Kashmir and Jericho Brown's poem, "Bullet Points," shared by several people in the last few days. While you know I am almost always wrestling with my general unhappiness at being stuck inside English, I do feel occasionally reconciled to this exiled state when I read certain poets. They remind me that it may still be possible to write challenging work within its confines. This poem, I feel, elevates English to a high degree – its authoritative voice and clarity of images make me think of Faiz's "Hum jo tarik rahon mein maarey gaye."[20] It deserves to be translated. I think an Urdu translation of this would be most salutary. 12:52 PM

I have been increasingly worried since the domicile law,[21] and we are hearing terrible news today. 10:32 AM

Dear Rahat, once again, please forgive me for the disappearing act. I hope you've had a relatively peaceful Eid and a fulfilling Ramadan.

Over the last month, I have slipped back to the place of despair and I am finding it increasingly difficult to hold on. Any hopes that I had entertained of the world ending have dissipated. It's been ten months of lockdown upon lockdown, a vertiginous loss of control that has dismantled the psychological structures of this place. My spaces of comfort in Kashmir over the last six years here were interstices that no longer exist. Now there is the overpowering scent of pale pink "Kashmir" roses that saturates every waking moment.

The light in Mr. Lanker's empty house is a scarecrow whose stare is matched by my brother's CCTV camera mounted right opposite. The two emptinesses watch over each other all day and all night and it makes me very, very sleepy.

I will be regaining access to my email next week, inshallah, when we get a better internet connection; I will also be able to access the record of our WhatsApp conversation. Please send any material you need me to read on my email.

I am at work today. Every road is seeped to the bone with desolation that reminds me of Ghalib's "Koi veerani si veerani hai / Dasht ko dekh ke ghar yaad aya,"[22] what with these being all peeling layers of a home lost time and again.

The stealing of Kashmir is final. Rahat, I have lived through three decades of this "war of attrition" and never before have I felt so sure about the death of the Resistance. These are the dead ashes of a conflict that has completely consumed Kashmir's psychic resources. There is nothing to be done. Reporting from the ground, dear Rahat, there is no more Kashmir.

Being trapped in the geographic limits of this place is like being stillborn – anew – every day. Enveloped in the terrible beauty of early summer, it sure smells like it ought to be someone's home. But here's also where so many are interred.

And then, of course, there is Black America. How timely is your recalling of Jericho Brown's "Bullet Points"! I attempted to translate it to Urdu, but it is a very ugly attempt, given my state of mind, although I am determined to try again, inshallah. The images of burning police precincts in Minneapolis are such a cooling sight to the eyes of those of us who are no longer even able to throw stones.

Last week I found a bunch of poems I wrote since August 2019, and I had forgotten that I'd written anything at all. I want to share them with you as part of this exchange of consciousnesses.

My mother has harvested the mint and she's
dried it in the sun and crushed it. 8:54 PM

2020-05-29

> Can you stay online awhile? I just woke up and had a
> feeling you might have written last night – 8:16 AM

Yes. I'm up for the next couple of hours. 8:46 PM

> All my other channels have gone quiet this week as if
> in anticipation of this, your latest dispatch. 8:16 AM

2020-05-30

Schrödinger's Therapy

The amaranthine thing about darkness
That it holds twice your weight in sorrow
which is to say,
it lives on

after it has swallowed you –
    nightshade
    moonflower
    hemlock
drunk on your bitterness
What the light doesn't, can't, won't touch
Is held sacred.

That it ferments grief;
For the body's vintage warehouse
Darkness holds;
Darkness holds you
So you may dwell
On the shoulder of the highway,
So you may mull over
That board of ephemera.

The thankful thing about darkness – the belly of the whale –
Is that it swallows you whole,
The integrity of your grief
    shame
    contradictions

Unchallenged by compulsive analytical clarity;
It adds nothing to you
And takes away nothing

It won't offer you tea, or coffee, or entertainment
Small talk, to make-yourself-at-home,

It makes room for each rib
And tenderly collapses around each lung
As you breathe.
It hones every raw nerve
Until fever smells like balsam

• • •

During fits of evanescent functionality
You leap madly across warp & weft
Lest the brain fog
Snag on a moment and unravel
That which never had a chance of being held.
You speak too much; you write too fast; you stumble over syllables
Anxious to outrun light
Fearful of being caught be-ing.
Light has no way to hold you
Without first weighing you

12:16 AM

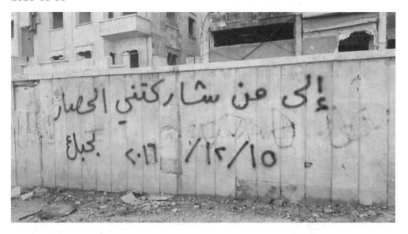

To the One Who Might Have Shared the Siege with Me

The world is full of walls:
Write to me

The imperative being made even more categorical
By this prime-number eternality
Indivisible into anything but itself
Indivisible into moons, ages, heartbeats,
Or other markers of scale;

By the Siege,
This humming, menacing monolith
suspended between space and time
Until the very texture of sand
Chokes the heart of the hourglass.

The world being full of sand,
You should have written to me,
Or at least counted the stars.
Breaths.
Blades of grass.
Shrapnel.
Anything to keep track of the silence.

Did you smoke the alphabet
Rolled up in columns of newsprint
Digits unsteady from too much (or not enough) sleep
Clawing at the city's white knuckles
Brittle as chalk

But while the city was full of chalk
You could have written to me.
All around us, the walls proliferated like mould –
Which is to say, they multiplied by long division
Or some other mathematical gimmick –
Walls
Without rooms
Walls
With a view
Walls
Worth their weight in pixels.

The universe is full of pixels;
You might have written to me. I think.
Plastered your heart to the curb
À la Banksy
And posted a picture of it to my wall –

Street Art, Graffiti, Tagging, Vandalism –
A *Missed Connection*, a *Tiny Love Story*
(You: besieged by circumstances.
Me: hemmed in by what wasn't around.
We made eye contact.
Call me if you read this.
The possibilities are endless.)

And what if you did, thereby,
And by some chronograph of desultory disposition,
Recalibrate the void
As the Aleppine lover did?

So although the city is still an unleavened loaf of bread,
The world is full of culture:

Although the body remains an unmarked mass grave,
The world is full of names:

And although the heart has always been a checkpointed,
barbed wire barrier along the Dead Sea shore,
The world is full of rubble:
Write to me.

April 25, 2020 / 1 Ramadan 1441. Belfry.

When sixteen, the body is a beehive
Seething with nectar, desire, hormones, neurochemicals
Plunging each into the other
Hunting for friction
Chasing each spark
As if fire itself were breath
And life
Highly flammable

At thirty-six, the body
Is a nest
Humming with echoes of silence
Muffled by a well-timed glance
A subsonic sigh,
A knowing, lingering caress
An oblique reference
Rustling, subtle as a breeze
The amber, the auburn
Crackling of the heart
As if blood were thick as water
And water
The essence of love

The river become the ocean
Oil-spilled
Lighthoused

Foghorned
Submarined
Expanse of hunger
Predator and prey at once
Bait and anchor
Empty and full
Regular, regulated
By phases of the moon

The menstrual cycle
Explains every heartache
Every soulmate.
Gangrene becomes self-aware
Love, then, a dialogue in meta-chemistry
When what is between the thighs
If not meditation

At sixteen, the body fills itself to the brim
A hallucinatory firework
An unburst bubble
Foaming at the mouth
With shadows;
The only explanatory power
Is vested in the skin's thousand eyes

Marriage primes, then perfects, the soul for loneliness
Snapping in half something
With the thinness and texture of a wafer biscuit
In the body's blue void
Lukewarm wine
Un-toastable

Divorce reassembles
Infidelities, indiscretions, intoxications, bones
Ashes, dust
Into a contraption
Rickety with too much purpose;
The heart, now afferent, greedy
Concentering
Upon the body pole-axed to focus desire

Like a magnifying glass

Indulgence
Melds into pain
In sultry gradations
Until what remains between the manifolds
Of the body
But camphor.

12:19 AM

Ghazal

"Roses for us and roses against us"[23]
The poet proposes; God disposes against us

Feelings that exist only in August:
An interminable summer reposes against us

Dust motes, lilac-lavendered midnights,
Time drowning out voices, when it flows, is against us

Who found the poem's skeleton along the foreshore
Ghazal-e-Farsi, reversed to prose, is against us

Jesus, is there nothing the darkness won't swallow?
A silhouette of loss: Suffering Moses against us[24]

The wheat-fragrant warmth of your hand on my forehead
Home a leavened dream the morning closes against us

One after each meal, one on an empty stomach:
Healing heartached by pills; and the dose is against us

The boys hurl roses from their slingshots on Fridays
How love perfumes Resistance, how revolution cozies against us!

The months feed on silence as if silence were a grain
Pain festering on pain, as it grows, is against us

Last night's raving vengeance snatched but two things:
My hope-darkened gaze, and the door that opens and closes against us

Light of My Eyes! You tipped a river into my cupped palms
But the ice in my chest, as our thirst froze, is against us

You were with me when the pines were with us
The moon rose with us; how it now glows is against us

Our garden of thorns is manicured to perfection
The wasp is in the thicket with the roses against us

12:23 AM

Ghazal

May peace be with you, O dwellers of graves
May your spirits malt in the vintage cellars of graves

In honour of our dead, we bury our hearts
The steady pulse of longing among the swellers of graves

When will that earthful of sleep seep into her bones
Night distilled unto night, tell her of graves?

Beneath the city you live in lies a phantom city:
Urban legend unearthed by the storytellers of graves

Between your history and my memory – a sprawling necropolis of desire
Unborn, unbearable bearers of names – two perfect little spellers of
    graves

(Did it or did it not die a fair death?
Exhume all evidence, call the expellers of graves)

The difference between wine and perfume is (that) of essence:
The halāl minus the harām, surplus blood on the hands of the sellers of
    graves

12:25 AM

2020-05-29

Sumayya, I have felt so different since I got to see you
and speak with you. I feel reconnected to the world –
that world which matters most to me – 5:48 PM

And if that, plus the renewed sense of momentum for our book that I have gained these last few days, weren't enough, you have sent me these poems.

It feels miraculous to read them. These ghazals! And your first poem – with its line about the belly of the whale – last fall I wrote the same line in an outpouring of bitterness if not resignation about this city.

Which I left unfinished. 5:50 PM

2020-05-31

Dear Sumayya, so much of what Kashmiris have been through is being re-enacted in the streets of U.S. cities these days. Bystanders being shot by rubber bullets. Journalists and photographers being tear-gassed, beaten, or threatened with beatings, and arrested. 3:10 PM

Aijaz texted me very early this morning, to ask my permission to go to today's anti-racism protest against the police murder of George Floyd. I was deeply moved by his comments. 6:48 PM

2020-06-09

Dear Rahat. 12:10 AM

The darkness balloons on the inside of my skull. Until I am not able to think of anything but destroying this body, this container of all pain. 12:11 AM

But it is a little funny that I've been so preoccupied with annihilating the self over the past three days. 12:13 AM

And trying at the same time to make a workable translation of "Bullet Points." I think I finally have a version that is not revolting. And reading it somehow tempers the drive to kill myself. 12:13 AM

نہ میں خود گولی اپنے سر میں مار کر
اور نہ ہی میں گولی اپنی کمر میں داغ کر
اور نہ ہی میں خود کو کوڑے کے تھیلے سے لٹکا کر
اپنی جان لوں گا
جولی بھی، تو میرا یہ وعدہ ہے
کہ پولیس کی گاڑی میں
ہتھکڑیوں میں بند ہو کے نہ کروں گا
نہ ایسے صوبے کے جیل خانے میں
جس کے نام سے میں صرف اس لئے واقف ہوں
کہ گھر آتے جاتے ادھر میرا گزر ہوتا ہے

:ہاں میں فروگیر تو ہوں، البتہ یہ جان لو
کہ کسی قانون کے محافظ کا اعتبار کرنے سے پہلے
میں اُن مکوڑوں کا اعتبار کر لوں
جو گھر کے فرش کی تختیوں کے نیچے پلتے ہیں
اور سڑتے مردار کے ساتھ طبقِ نیاز سلوک کرتے ہیں

اِس ملک کے قانون کے محافظ سے تو میری اتنی بھی امید نہیں
کہ مرتے دم میری آنکھیں ایک خدا شناس بندے کی طرح بند کرے
یا پھر مجھے ایک چادر ہی اوڑھائے
جو اتنی صاف تو ہو کہ میری ماں اس میں مجھے سلائے

جب میں اپنی جان لے لوں گا
:تو بس ویسے ہی لوں گا جیسے امریکیوں کی ریت ہے
،سگریٹ کے دھوئیں سے
،یا گوشت کے ایک ٹکڑے کے میرے گلے میں اٹک جانے سے
یا پھر مفلسی کی اس قدر شدت سے
کہ یخ بستہ سردیوں میں ٹھٹھر کر چل بسوں

جو تمہیں میری موت کی خبر یوں ہوئی
کہ پولیس کا کوئی اہلکار میرے نزدیک ہوا
تو سن رکھو کہ وہی پولیس والا میرا قاتل ہے
وہی ہے جس نے میرے جسم کو رہا کر
مجھے ہمارے بیچ میں سے چھینا ہے
اور جیسا کہ ہم دیکھ چکے ہیں
یہ بات کسی بھی تصفئے سے بڑھ کر ہے
اس فدیہ سے جو قاضیانِ شہر میری ماں کو پیش کریں گے

تاکہ وہ رونا دھونا بند کرے
اور یہ بات اس گولی سے بھی زیادہ سوزنا ک ہے
جسے میرے دماغ کی تہوں میں سے برآمد کیا جائے گا

12:15 AM

I have failed to find a suitable idiomatic translation of
the title, though, something that might do justice to
both meanings. For now, I think it may be best to just
transliterate it. So that it is "Bullet Points" in Urdu. I will
soon send you a Romanized Urdu version. 12:16 AM

2020-06-08

> Dear Sumayya, yes, the closeness to the essentials
> of language that this work requires has its
> own volition – its own life force. 11:57 AM

> You wrote me earlier about having read Jhumpa Lahiri's
> *In Other Words* – I believe you must have read it during
> the Months – or anyway not long ago. 11:58 AM

> And in the moment I couldn't say how much that
> book – that transformative process that Lahiri
> gave herself up to – affected me … 11:59 AM

> gave me something – a channel for imagining my own
> escape – in a way no monolingual writer can. 12:03 PM

> Before this, her fiction has also represented the kind
> of world-making that stirred my ambitions to write
> literary criticism – it actually helped to illuminate
> for me what literature is for and why I cling to
> language in the ways I have done … 12:05 PM

2020-06-08

> **Romanized Urdu Version of Jericho Brown's "Bullet Points"**

> Na meiñ khud goli apne sar meiñ mār kar
> Aur na hē meiñ goli apni kamar meiñ daagh kar
> Aur na hē meiñ khud ko kūdéy ké thailéy sé latkā kar
> Apnī jān lūñga
> Jo lī bhī, tô méra yeh wāda hai
> Ki police kī gādī meiñ

Hath-kadioñ meiñ band ho ke na karūñga
Na aisé sūbey kay jail-khāney meiñ
Jis ke nām sé meiñ sirf isliyé wāqif hoūñ
Ke ghar ātéy-jātéy udhar mérā guzar hotā hai

Hāñ meiñ farū-gīr toh hoūñ, albatta yeh jān lo:
Ke kisī qānūn kay muhāfiz kā aitbār karné sé pehlay
Meiñ un makodoñ kā aitbār kar loūñ
Jo ghar kay farsh kī takhtiyoñ kay nīchay paltay haiñ
Ki sadtey murdār kay sāth tabq-e-niyāz sulūk kartay haiñ

Iss mulk kay qānūn kay muhāfiz sé toh mérī itnī bhī umīd nahīñ
Ke martay damm mérī āñkhéñ ék khudā-shanās banday kī tarah bannd
    karey
Yā phir mujhé ék chādar hē ōdhāyé
Jo itnī sāf toh ho ke mérī māñ us meiñ mujhé sulā sakey

Jab meiñ apnī jān lénéy pé āoūñga
Toh bas waisé hē loūñgā jaisey Amrīkiyoñ kī rīt hai:
Yā toh cigarette kay dhuéñ sé,
Yā gosht kay ék niwālay kay méréy galéy meiñ atak jāné sé,
Yā phir muflisī kī iss qadr shiddat sé
Ke yakh-basta sardiyoñ meiñ thithur kar chal basoūñ

Jo tumheiñ mérī maut kī khabar yoūñ huī
Ke police kā koī ahlkār méréy nazdīk huā
Toh sun rakho ke wahī police wālā mérā qātil hai.
Wahī hai jis né méréy jism ko rihā kar
Mujhé hamāréy bīch sé chīnā hai
Aur jaisā ke ham dékh chukéy haiñ
Yeh bāt kisī bhī tasfiyé sé badh kar hai
Uss fidyé sé jo qāziyān-e-shahr méri māñ ko pésh karéñgé
Tāke woh ronā-dhonā bannd karéy
Aur yeh bāt uss golī sé bhī zyāda sūz-nāk hai
Jiséy méréy dimāgh kī tahoñ meiñ sé barāmad kiyā jāyégā

12:43 AM

2020-06-08

Thank you so much for doing this
work, dear Sumayya. 12:13 PM

2020-06-09

Thank you, Rahat, for bringing me to do this.
There is so much relief in it. 12:47 AM

2020-06-08

> I thought of you immediately as soon as
> I read it. Alhamdulillah, for whatever in
> this world brings you relief. 12:18 PM

2020-06-09

Re: the drive to inhabit multiple languages or at least to have
them live in us. After we spoke about your belongingness in
languages the last time, I wanted to learn French. I think I
have always hated how it sounds. And perhaps what it has
always concealed from me. In a maddening way where the
letters seem to be a language I *ought to* know but the words
and the sentences are locked beyond reach. 12:49 AM

I just started a Duolingo course in French. 😄 12:51 AM

And the little green owl manipulates me. But I have to
do its bidding. I don't want to let it down. 😄 12:52 AM

2020-06-08

> Mubarak aur félicitations! 12:24 PM

2020-06-09

Hahaha merci! 12:54 AM

2020-06-08

> When I went to Montréal in 2016 to read from
> *Cosmophilia*, I also wrote a short prose narrative in
> French about a photograph of my mother taken in that
> city in 1969. And the feeling of giddiness that I had when
> I was writing it – when I felt it take shape in my head in
> the French – is the same feeling I recognized in Lahiri's
> account of when she began writing secretly in Italian.
> The most exhilarating, lawless freedom. 12:35 PM

2020-06-09

I would love to work on deciphering it. 1:08 AM

> I also wrote a poem in French in 2017. In mourning for the Québec City mosque massacre – and as a rebuke that was also completely spontaneous –
>
> I want to spend a bit of time with your translation … and your idea for the title is best. 12:40 PM

I rarely feel as satisfied with a translation as I find myself feeling with this. 2:03 AM

I struggled with Jericho Brown's quiet, measured rage and tried to reconcile it with the truth of my own helplessness. 2:10 AM

> It's a cool June evening of rain and fresh green-infused air. I went out to shake off the grey and gather some roses for you and your niece. 6:57 PM

> Dear Sumayya, I finally looked up the story your poem responds to, about the spray-painted dedication on the Aleppo wall. The detestable BuzzFeed makes two quick bites of it – quickly consumed and forgotten. 12:36 PM
>
> Your response is the true response. 12:46 PM
>
> It occurs to me that no one could have done poetic justice to the story except you. Partly because of the high akhlaq of your sensibility as a poet. But also the authority of your position – the bodily reality of being held in siege, under a communication blockade, while you wrote it. No one outside that reality should even try to touch this topic. No one else has the right. And as I said the other night, the fact that your refrain comes from Shahid, stranded without a post office, elevates this poem beyond one of simple romantic longing and stakes it to new literary ground altogether. I am thrilled that it is going to enter the Kashmiri literary lineage. 12:54 PM

Dear Raḥat. I am very much not okay. Please make du'ā for me. I will respond to your kind messages as soon as I'm better. 🖤 8:52 PM

> Dear Sumayya, it doesn't matter if you can't reply to me yet, I know that you want to when you are able. I will intensify my du'a. Call me if you think talking would help. Or I can call you. 9:45 AM

> It was a golden evening here last night and I went for a long walk. I saw this white iris: 9:46 AM

Thank you for flowers. 10:17 PM

> The evenings are very long here – the sky was still clear blue at 10 p.m. last night. 10:08 AM

Oh, I remember those interminable June
evenings of Vancouver. 10:39 PM

> Yes. Mine was only relieved by Aijaz coming home
> just a bit before me. So at least we were able to sit
> together and eat together. He is still asleep. 10:10 AM

> Last night, I read a bit of the history book on Indo-
> Persian poetry by Sunil Sharma, called *Mughal
> Arcadia*.[25] I think I would have enjoyed a seventeenth-
> century life working in a kitab khana. There are so
> many illuminated manuscripts or folios that have
> ended up in the British Museum – honestly its name
> should be changed to Cool Stuff We Stole. 10:19 AM

> Sleep well. If you aren't able to sleep let
> me know. I will call you. 10:42 AM

2020-06-13

Dear Rahat, I fell asleep soon after. Thank you for putting up
with my flightiness. I woke up fatigued, with body aches and
chills. One of my colleagues with whom I am routinely in
close contact tested positive for the coronavirus last week. I
am isolating myself at home. Or at least supposed to. 1:45 PM

Because apparently my boss doesn't give a fuck. 1:46 PM

He twice called me in to work while I clearly stated I
was in quarantine, having been in close contact with
the colleague who is confirmed positive. 1:47 PM

This despite the so-called Government of India "guidelines"
on restricting the spread of the virus. 1:48 PM

When I protested he said I ought to maintain a positive
spirit and not find ways to not attend duties. 1:49 PM

He said I'd be alright, I just need to be a little brave. 1:50 PM

It's amazing what delusions masculinity
can lead you into. 1:50 PM

He said that even he was feeling "a bit of a sore
throat" but 🌶 "work is work." 1:52 PM

And the urgent "work" that he needed me to attend to was to draft a posthumous letter of appointment for another colleague who just passed away three days ago. 1:53 PM

My disrespect for and disgust with authority and institutions has officially lost its bottom. 1:54 PM

This is a strange summer in Srinagar, climate-wise. 1:55 PM

It's much cooler than usual, although still perfectly sunny in the day. And in the late afternoon to early evenings it regularly rains, and that reminds me of my time in KL. 1:56 PM

How I miss KL rains! 1:56 PM

I didn't know rain and rain could be so different. 1:57 PM

There's KL rain and there's Vancouver rain. 1:57 PM

Vancouver rain makes you want to destroy something, preferably yourself. 1:57 PM

This summer rain in Srinagar is bringing me much-needed peace, something I never thought was possible. I actually look forward to it. 1:59 PM

Am I suddenly one of those people who find the rain aesthetically pleasing and call themselves "pluviophile" in their Instagram bios? 2:00 PM

I have always been almost militant in my hatred of it. 2:31 PM

But these brief, light showers are new. 2:31 PM

I'm not sure what about them manages to get to me. 2:31 PM

Months upon months upon months of spending time with the same seven people must be driving me insane. 2:32 PM

Oh Rahat, as I was practising French on the app, my niece, she of the emotional genius (keeper of the keys to everyone's heart), overheard. She was upset and said I shouldn't be learning French because it's a rude language. 2:35 PM

She'd heard the app repeatedly tell me "tu parles" and her Urdu ears heard "tu pagal hai" ["you're crazy"]. 2:36 PM

2:36 PM

Dear Rahat, I am happy with the title you've chosen, given Shahid is kind of a starting point in our individual journeys into poetry and the confluence of poetry and Kashmir and the urban condition. I have gone through the manuscript. It is amazing how consistent some things have remained over the years. Yet also how much "scatter" there is. 11:20 PM

Thank you for writing to me during the Months. 11:23 PM

2020-06-15

Dear Sumayya, the pink flamingos have landed, having carried several titles of contemporary Persian poetry from Toronto, with a collection of poems by Attieh Attarzadeh, "the wound you inherit from the earth." My friend Khashayar has also translated some of her poems and inserted them into the paperback. 6:39 PM

Grateful for the light, dear Rahat. Also, I love the
pink flamingos and haven't been able to stop thinking
about them ever since I saw that (Cath Kidston–like?)
print that I woke up to this morning. 9:47 PM

I used to have a PE instructor in high school who would come
into the classroom on days when it rained and we couldn't
have our drills in the schoolyard. He had such perfect Urdu
penmanship (even with chalk on blackboard). 9:49 PM

He was an older guy whom I always think very fondly
of. Although he had a rather "military" demeanour and
no one in my fourth grade of girls liked him. 10:12 PM

On rainy days when he'd walk into the classroom, everyone
would quietly hope for him to go away. 10:14 PM

But he so pointedly always did either of
two things on those days. 10:14 PM

Either he'd give us math problems to solve (again in
perfect penmanship on the blackboard) … 10:14 PM

Or he'd write a poetic riddle in Urdu … 10:15 PM

With zero context … 10:15 PM

And expect this mass of very scared girls to tell
him what it meant. I mean, my generation wasn't
particularly great at Urdu, but in fourth grade, poetry
at my school was at best Islamic nasheeds. 10:16 PM

He never concealed his disappointment – almost
disgust – with how bad we were in Urdu. 10:17 PM

He said, "Kya khaak urdu parhte ho tum!" 10:17 PM

One of those riddles – which your pink flamingos have
brought back in some kind of inexplicable déjà vu – was this:

بگلا کا سر کاٹ کر اس کے پاؤوں میں رکھ دو

یہ چیز ایک دوست نے دوسرے دوست سے مانگی تھی

10:19 PM

I was infinitely fascinated by this play on words. 10:20 PM

Somewhere in my ten-year-old brain, I knew it was a play on words even though I couldn't guess the answer. 10:21 PM

He gave us a COMPLETE hour of silence to think it over. 😂 10:21 PM

At the end of the period he said the answer was گلاب. 10:22 PM

And "kya khaak urdu parhte ho tum!"[26] 10:22 PM

May God bless his soul and surround him with His peace. Even though the prospect of chopping off a flamingo's head is a little off-putting. 10:22 PM

> Yes, the tone and expression are a fitting use for the instrument of Urdu. 9:56 AM
>
> Baglā = flamingo? 9:57 AM

I think it's a heron, but here the flamingo will stand in, no? 😊 10:28 PM

2020-06-21

Solstice mubarak, dear Rahat. We're having a ring eclipse today. Ayaan nearly broke down the door to my room. So excited. 12:15 PM

2020-06-20

> How are you feeling? 11:46 PM

2020-06-21

I am feeling quite down since last night. 12:16 PM

How are you? 12:16 PM

2020-06-20

> I am all right. It was a grey solstice here, with a warm rain that I personally wouldn't have minded lasting

longer. But I went downtown for the first time in over three months, to meet the restricted number of friends for zikr because I felt as if the walls of my apartment were closing in. My throat was parched either from not being used to live conversation or maybe because there is a lot of pollen in the air.

By the way, one of the women who is a new member of the Unity zikr circle comes from France. She asked me about my writing, and that reminded me I intended to send you this. Its meaning will not elude you for very long. 11:47 PM

Après Sainte-Foy 2 / Laïcité

Ne me parle pas d'amour ce soir; ne me parle pas de foi.
Ce sont des mots qui glissent aisément à la surface de notre méfiance.
De ce jardin enchevêtré que j'ai assemblé avec ma poésie, je ne serai
  jamais déplacée.

Ce soir je reconnais les éléments de la foi qui ont fourni les éléments de
  ton doute,
et l'espace entre les deux où, autrefois, on pouvait jouer
et l'espace entre les deux, rempli de tout ce qui n'est pas encore nommé;
de tout ce qui n'a jamais eu besoin d'un nom.

le 29 janvier 2017

11:52 PM

2020-06-27

Dear Rahat, on Thursday morning I pulled a power cord around my neck in one more unsuccessful attempt to put out this dumpster fire of a life. Failure won't leave me alone, even in death. Or maybe – and this is more likely – I'm just a coward, doomed to some kind of eternity that the religiously minded call hell. 6:54 PM

Please send anything that might make this more bearable until it passes. 6:57 PM

Thank you for telling me this. 8:57 AM

I thank God for what you call your failure. 9:00 AM

I grieve for your sake. That the pain has come
back for you so viciously like this. 9:04 AM

I was rereading your segment from earlier this year
when you described your experience at Umrah.
The clean-burning anger in your lines. 9:15 AM

I know that healing ebbs and flows,
dear Sumayya. 9:21 AM

It is one of the injustices for which I
frequently rage at God. 9:21 AM

During this winter I kept thinking that I needed
the anger to leave my body. 9:22 AM

But at least, the clarity of my anger
keeps me awake. 9:23 AM

I wouldn't wish it on you – I wouldn't wish it on anyone –
my anger has been returning to me in dreams. 9:24 AM

So I know that life will not suddenly become
simple and singular. Anger is not done with me.
And now reading your message and confronting
the thought of you being in that much pain – I
see I am far from done with anger. 9:29 AM

If there is anything else I can do to help you fight
this that you can think of, please tell me. 10:06 AM

2020-06-30

I have reached that point, in this 2020 Zombie Apocalypse
Pandemic, of a restless craving for the life of the city.

But when I leave my door, I want the cobblestones
of Rome or Florence or Venice to step out onto.

I want the spotless high-speed Shinkansen to pull
me across the island from Tokyo to Kyoto.

I want to follow Bob Odenkirk's earnestly no-good loser
with a cut-rate law degree as he slips out the back of a
building on the outskirts of Albuquerque and walks into
the hot desert light on the trail of some mystery. I can't
remember the name of the character he plays because he
lies to almost everyone he meets and frequently changes
his name. But the ribbons of light across the desert sky
and its heat and silence have a fidelity to them, abiding
fidelity, sufficient for me and my craving to wander.

I want to browse the bookstalls of old Lahore on a Friday
and stay up all night listening to the grandchildren
of my mother's aunt tell ghost stories. And I want to
see the Siachen Glacier. I will wear tall black fur-lined
boots with ice grips on their soles and I will whip all
the army generals who played at war with the lives of
boys. I will do it on behalf of their bereft mothers – it
would be the least courtesy I could show them – and
give my deepest salam to the mountain peaks.

I have been dreaming of mountain peaks, dear
Sumayya – but in my most recent vivid dream I
was looking down at a mountain – horizontally
striped with purple – contained inside a clear lake,
inside a crater. The crater was vast and folded into
a gap amid such high peaks – a voice beckoned
me forward from a group of trees to a clearing of
stone, a narrow lookout over an amazing vista –

I want to travel back in time to the late eighteenth century
and see Guangzhou and take a boat up the Pearl River
and watch silk weavers and calligraphers. 3:11 PM

And I also want to go by boat to Melaka to hear
the melee of multiple languages spoken by all the
traders swarming into the port. And I want to see
Lake Baikal in Siberia. It is said to be the oldest and
deepest freshwater lake in the world. 3:41 PM

If I can't go to any of these places, then I want
it to be 1991 so I can be twenty-one years old

in New York City. I would go to all the indie gallery art openings and free rock concerts and write sharp reviews about them all. 3:49 PM

Here in the cool grey last day of June I don't even really want particularly to go downtown to pick up the book I ordered. I don't want the ordinariness of going to a store. 4:02 PM

I don't believe that anything should go back to being the same. The effort seems disastrous, dishonest. 4:04 PM

But I still made a hair appointment for later this week. Vanity must assert itself somewhere in my restlessness. 4:28 PM

2020-07-01

Dear Rahat, thank you for composing Hankering after A Composite City in this conversation. I can't stop reading the lines over and over again. Despite the haunting and the nostalgia, the urgency lends it a lightweight tone that is almost hopeful. Maps of cities and times superimposed on each other ... 2:23 PM

Representing a singular craving. 2:24 PM

Not just for the not-here & not-now but for everything the body is already primed for. I love it. 2:25 PM

Dear Sumayya, thank you for reading and naming my cravings. 10:42 AM

The overdetermined first of July colonial holiday was satisfyingly rainy and cold. 9:45 PM

2020-07-02

It is grey and cold again today. I sip my coffee, and I survey my domain. 12:40 PM

I survey my domain, with a critical, a calculating eye. 12:41 PM

For the shelf life of books and papers may soon expire. 12:42 PM

I feel an oncoming will power. A woman with a room of her own – a whole apartment, in fact – is a formidable thing. A space I have lived in – existed, subsisted – for more than fifteen years now and which I might inhabit for only a limited time more. 12:46 PM

I would like to invite you to join me in this game, dear Sumayya. Let's call it my Zamindāri. 1:27 PM

Where the law grants me absolute ownership, and over which I may exercise the most absolute, uncompromising control. 1:29 PM

2020-07-03

This most gracious & empowering invitation I accept with the spirit of our Grandmothers' ownership of Earth and its land. 5:03 AM

Thank you. Remembering the Grandmothers will guide me as I exorcise the demons of this square footage and prepare to expel the lie … 5:07 PM

That encased my life in its smooth shell for so many years. 5:10 PM

That's it … the lie that forms the core of all subsequent regret and self-loathing. 5:49 AM

The lie that makes everything look too perfect. 5:50 AM

May the truth of your own ownership & control heal you … 5:50 AM

While you hold your domain. 5:51 AM

Ameen. 5:22 PM

2020-07-05

Based on your preferred chocolate, I bought a Kit Kat bar for my next-door neighbour – I was returning her small dessert plate and wanted something to put in it. 2:33 PM

Yesterday she presented me with a full dish of cooked noodles and chicken. 2:33 PM

It's like the Christian fishes and loaves story … 2:34 PM

Except with a Kit Kat, between a
Buddhist and a Muslim. 2:34 PM

2020-07-06

Dear Rahat, I'm so happy that Kit Kat has a place in
your chocolate repertoire. I love the idea of exchange
of food. It is so elemental to community. 1:41 PM

And may God bring the same kind of barakah to your
exchange of food as He did with feeding the multitude. 1:44 PM

And finally – I may have some good news
on the romantic front. 1:46 PM

I am meeting with an incredibly gracious man
who has no grandiose promises. 1:47 PM

I am hopeful … 1:47 PM

Although also terribly wary, as you know. 1:47 PM

Please make du'ā for me as I seriously consider
this person for a future. 1:48 PM

2020-07-10

What have you decided, sha'ir sahiba? 3:32 PM

2020-07-11

The ayes have it, dear Rahat. 9:28 AM

2020-07-18

I keep rereading your "roses against us" ghazal. 10:34 AM

It makes me want to take pre-emptive action against
the feelings that exist only in August. 10:35 AM

2020-07-22

Dear Sumayya, have you come across the
French word for "nightmare" yet? 10:14 PM

"Cauchemar" might amuse you, as a homonym. 10:15 PM

(I thought of it while looking at Google Maps ... there is a town or village called Kāshmar in Iran.) 10:37 PM

2020-07-24

Dear Sumayya, this is the view from the park bench where I spent some time rereading Suvir Kaul's *Of Gardens and Graves* this afternoon: 11:34 PM

2020-07-24

The photo appearance of the vaulted sky much more dramatic than I expected – reminds me of mid-century CinemaScope movies – it looks unreal. But I was really there, reading about the established formal structure of the ghazal in tension with trauma and alienation as collective experience written by Kashmiri poets. 11:36 PM

2020-07-25

Dear Sumayya, political chatter among the self-important & the saboteurs is getting louder. I'd really like to see you & hear how you are. May I please call you tonight? It will be your Sunday morning. 1:09 PM

2020-07-26

Dear Rahat, please forgive the radio silence. A couple of medical crises in the family. I would love to talk, inshallah. Will confirm. 6:39 AM

Oh, sorry I was thinking my Sunday evening. Is that feasible? I am at the hospital right now and will be home by evening. 6:40 AM

2020-07-25

Try calling me here when you can. We'll figure it out. 6:19 PM

2020-07-26

Okay. 6:51 AM

2020-07-31

Should I forward you the mandatory sheep meme? I had the pleasure of waking up to one, among several Eid messages this morning. 12:19 PM

2020-08-02

How is your aunt, dear Sumayya? How is your exhausted uncle? Please let me know. 10:45 AM

Dear Rahat, Eid mubarak … Maami is stable although still quite hopeless in terms of surgery. My fiancé, meanwhile, has tested positive. 11:16 PM

Oh no! 10:47 AM

Can't seem to catch a breath. 11:17 PM

Is your fiancé able to stay in isolation? 10:49 AM

Yes, alhamdulillah he's isolated. 11:19 PM

With minimal symptoms. 11:20 PM

The apocalypse is a little more dramatic than I had imagined it would be. 11:22 PM

Honestly. I am just thankful to have this connection with the only sense of home I have. I think these circumstances are all so entirely obstreperous. 10:57 AM

This week the hindutva goons are going to invade Times Square in NYC with a live broadcast from Ayodhya ... 10:57 AM

And I'm beside myself. I keep thinking of what you said about how they stole your summer – the Kashmiri summer. 10:58 AM

These acts of theft are proving to be an addiction for them. 10:59 AM

So our book constitutes a very definitive resistance. We will hurl our verses, dear Sumayya. 11:00 AM

Inshallah, thank you for giving me this connection beyond the hackneyed rhetoric. 11:31 PM

That has invaded even poetry. 11:31 PM

Ugh. 11:02 AM

I know. 11:02 AM

This field of the intimate is probably the last refuge of the traumatized. 11:32 PM

I hope it will be so for those of us ... 11:33 PM

Who are uprooted yet trapped ... 11:33 PM

Isolated yet crowded out. 11:33 PM

I might have mentioned that earlier this spring, I found two handwritten poems at the backs of some old notebooks from before *Cosmophilia* was published.

Invention

I see it –

If no angel ever embraced
Muhammad in the cave of Hira
nearly crushing his ribs –

If no angel announced
the Virgin Birth

to fall upon Mary –

If Ibrahim never built the Kaaba
If Noah never built the Ark

If a body draped in white
or black fabric signalled
neither a bride of heaven
nor descent from a prophet;

I see how I would
have had to invent it all myself;

Milton, Shakespeare, Donne, Attar, Hafez;
the serpent, the golden apples
the exultation, the damnation
the rungs of the ladder
the rungs of the ladder

I would have had to invent
the patrician heart of Ghazali and
the effulgent blasphemy of Hallaj and

the chocolate and the cinnamon
the chocolate and the cinnamon

the Aztec rites honouring
the Lady of the Dead

I would have had to invent
the first people to hear revelation

and the mountains refused to hear it
because they would have crumbled under its blast

I would have had to invent
the arts of summoning
every wrathful or timid jinn

For a curse to bear meaning,
to curse you with enough force

I would have had to invent
the sirat for an almighty Hu

to burst forth from my heart,
to reveal Hu's dwelling place –

to call down enough wrath upon you

11:06 AM

Love of Ornament Is Also Love of Order / Fool's Gold

Let the setting sun catch my gold.
Let fine lines on me briefly gleam,
like an October hour that recalls

whole August days. I still need
to write this need to adorn I inherited
from women – to write: Adornment –

legible only when shared –
as ritual induction into lineage
requires a room of its own

One grandmother, at least two aunts

one to frown *hold still*, blending colour
onto your cheekbones; another to recognize,
pleased, *aren't those the bangles I gave you?*

Circles and chains, silver and gold
speak not history but living bonds;
years of Eids and birthdays; girls

becoming women
among their women;
proofs of fidelity –

against a future
that keeps its promises

to no one, anywhere, ever.

Circles and chains remain,
when living bonds drop away.
What meaning remains?

I fear death less
the more I recognize

the gnawing
inside the woman

who goes gazing at fool's gold

who rifles through old trinkets
in search of a lost self –

the butterfly ring in silver filigree
Safa sent, just for friendship –

the stamped brass earrings
in the shape of birds
that drew compliments
at dinner parties

and held my baby son's gaze
when I held him in my arms.

I spotted this ring of bright yellow resin
in a store window, on a winter night

I use it to coax my amygdala
into believing I've trapped sunlight –

ring that clicks against the key
when I lock the door to a silent home.

when I twist and pull
with my restless fingers
at iron pyrite on a chain –

iron pyrite, shiny rocks
I shopped for alone
shiny rocks that speak
no sentiment
and tell no story

except a cheque I got
for some poems.

And I also have a drawing I made of my Nani while she recited poetry. During her last couple of years on earth. 11:06 AM

Dukh bhi aa jaye tho ho dil na parreshaan mera.
Ke sihukar hawr haal me ho
Meri zubaan par thera
Allama Iqbal, recited by Jahmida Begum
Drawn live by Rahat Kurd
Saturday, January 19 2013

Oh my God! 11:37 PM

You did mention the poems but not the drawing I think. 11:37 PM

These documents ... 11:41 PM

Fragments of conversations ... 11:41 PM

Salvaged from distance ... 11:41 PM

Relics stolen from time ... 11:42 PM

It's these documents ... 11:44 PM

That form our resistance ... 11:45 PM

To all kinds of tyranny. 11:45 PM

> Yes. I feel this way about your handwritten letters. 11:15 AM

> And the exchange we had about the designer Guo Pei's gowns and the kanni jung. 11:16 AM

Oh, I still look at those pictures of shoes sometimes. 11:47 PM

> Fixing this image of my grandmother while she recited was exactly that, an act of defiance against time's wreckage. 11:17 AM

> And I still think about your custom-designed pheran. 11:18 AM

Oh, Rahat I wanted this to be a surprise, but since the world is ending I'm not sure how things will work out ... I made a pheran for you ... 11:49 PM

Which I was hoping to send you. 11:49 PM

I'm still hoping to. 11:49 PM

> This news makes me so happy. Please hold on to it for me. The world will have to stop ending for us. Your fiancé will have to get well, inshallah, and you will have to get married, and find some happiness. 11:20 AM

> This too makes a powerful resistance. In the very teeth of the apocalypse. 11:21 AM

Please hex the multiple occupations. 11:51 PM

> I will. I think the sisters of the Musqueam, Squamish, and Tsleil-Waututh Nations will not object if I burn cedar and sage and invoke the divine feminine against the colonizers ... 11:22 AM

> And inshallah I will come get the pheran from you in person. 11:59 AM

Endnotes

1   Suvir Kaul, *Of Gardens and Graves: Kashmir, Poetry, Politics*, photographs by Javed Dar (Durham, NC: Duke University Press, 2017).

2   "Dargah" as a generic noun refers to a shrine, but in Srinagar, the entire residential-commercial district that surrounds the shrine where the Prophet's relic is supposed to be located is named "Dargah" for administrative purposes.

3   Included in Rahat Kurd's *Cosmophilia* (Vancouver, BC: Talonbooks, 2015).

4   Helen Vendler and Emily Dickinson, *Dickinson: Selected Poems and Commentaries* (Cambridge, MA: Belknap Press of Harvard University Press, 2010).

5   Song by Sajjad Hussain and Rajendra Krishan, notably sung by Talat Mahmood.

6   See www.hollyschmidt.ca / all-the-trees.

7   Included in Rahat Kurd's *Cosmophilia*.

8   Included in *The Mirror of My Heart: A Thousand Years of Persian Poetry by Women*, trans. Dick Davis (Odenton, MD: Mage Publishers, 2019).

9   A guest editorship on the theme "What Does It Mean to Be a Muslim Writer?" for the *Puritan* online literary magazine. Published June 2019.

10   This poem quotes the famous opening line from Charlotte Brontë's *Jane Eyre* and al-Qur'ān 13:41.

11   Vigils were held on the evening of March 15 in Vancouver and around the world to mourn for the fifty-one people killed by a

white supremacist at two mosques in Ōtautahi (Christchurch), Aotearoa (New Zealand).

12   Anne Carson, "First Choral Ode from *Norma Jeane Baker of Troy* (A Translation of Euripides' *Helen*)," *London Review of Books* 41, no. 7 (March 7, 2019).

13   Feminist writers have argued that use of "aurat" in Urdu is inherently patriarchal and privileges an objectifying, chauvinistic definition, spelled out in Sumayya's reply: "that which must be concealed."

14   Rukhsana Ahmad, trans. and ed., *We Sinful Women: Contemporary Urdu Feminist Poetry* (London, UK: Women's Press, 1991).

15   These poems were first published in the *Puritan* online literary magazine, June 26, 2019, in the "What Does It Mean to Be a Muslim Writer" issue, guest-edited by Rahat Kurd.

16   Agha Shahid Ali, "Return to Harmony 3," *The Country without a Post Office: Poems* (New York, NY: W.W. Norton, 1997).

17   From a poem by Faiz Ahmed Faiz popularly known as "Ham Dekhenge" (We shall see).

18   Come, let us, too, raise our hands in prayer
Those of us who do not know the ritual of the supplication
Those of us who, besides remembering the scorching buzz of love,
Remember no other idol, no other god
(from Faiz Ahmed Faiz, "Dua," translation by Sumayya Syed)

19   We have neither a license to our weapon, nor power
That we may fight the enemy of Turkey;
So we curse, from the bottom of our heart:
May worms infest the cannons of Italy!
(translation by Sumayya Syed)

20   "We who were murdered in the darkest lanes."

21   Jammu and Kashmir's official semi-autonomous statehood, while actively undermined through thirty years of military occupation, was at least protected in the letter of the law (article 370 of the Indian constitution). After its August 5, 2019, abrogation of that

article, the BJP regime's new domicile law followed in 2020, unilaterally opening up Kashmiri land and potential development contracts to non-Kashmiris, leaving Kashmiris no representation at a state level and no recourse to protect either their land or their sovereignty.

22 "I wondered if any wilderness would be more desolate than this! And then I remembered another of the kind – the home I'd left behind" (translation by Sumayya Syed).

23 Mahmoud Darwish, "We Journey towards a Home," *Unfortunately, It Was Paradise: Selected Poems*, trans. Munir Akash and Carolyn Forché, ed. Sinan Antoon and Amira El-Zein (Oakland, CA: University of California Press, 2013).

24 Suffering Moses is the name of a store selling Kashmiri handicrafts and artifacts on the Bund in Srinagar.

25 Sunil Sharma, *Mughal Arcadia: Persian Literature in an Indian Court* (Cambridge, MA: Harvard University Press, 2017).

26 "What worthless Urdu you have studied!"

Works Cited

Ali, Agha Shahid. *The Country without a Post Office: Poems*. New York, W.W. Norton: 1997.

—. "Snowmen." *The Half-Inch Himalayas*. Middletown, CT: Wesleyan University Press, 1987.

Ahmad, Rukhsana, trans. and ed. *We Sinful Women: Contemporary Urdu Feminist Poetry*. London, UK: Women's Press, 1991.

Carson, Anne. "First Choral Ode from *Norma Jeane Baker of Troy* (A Translation of Euripides' *Helen*)," *London Review of Books* 41, no. 7 (March 7, 2019).

Cavafy, C.P. "The City." *Selected Poems*. Translated by David Connolly. Athens, Greece: Aiora Press, 2015.

Darwish, Mahmoud. "We Journey towards a Home." *Unfortunately, It Was Paradise: Selected Poems*. Translated by Munir Akash and Carolyn Forché. Edited by Sinan Antoon and Amira El-Zein. Oakland, CA: University of California Press, 2013.

Davis, Dick, trans. *The Mirror of My Heart: A Thousand Years of Persian Poetry by Women*. Odenton, MD: Mage Publishers, 2019.

Kaul, Suvir. *Of Gardens and Graves: Kashmir, Poetry, Politics*. Photographs by Javed Dar. Durham, NC: Duke University Press, 2017.

Kurd, Rahat. *Cosmophilia*. Vancouver, BC: Talonbooks, 2015.

Sharma, Sunil. *Mughal Arcadia: Persian Literature in an Indian Court*. Cambridge, MA: Harvard University Press, 2017.

Vendler, Helen, and Emily Dickinson. *Dickinson: Selected Poems and Commentaries*. Cambridge, MA: Belknap Press of Harvard University Press, 2010.

Permissions

Acknowledgments

While this work was in progress, the voices of many writers kept me company with their solace and reassurance in pushing the boundaries of narrative form: Rebecca Solnit, Edward Said, John Berger, Lauren Elkin, Miriam Toews, Mahmoud Darwish and his translators, Ibrahim Muhawi and Carolyn Forché, and Nitasha Kaul and Ather Zia, in whose co-edited volume *Can You Hear Kashmiri Women Speak? Narratives of Resistance and Resilience* (2020) the anthropologist and Kashmiri Pandit writer Nishita Trisal poignantly writes of trauma and the Pandit–Muslim impasse, making "a plea to find a way to one another again, to understand what we have lost, and what might yet remain for us to save."

Heartfelt thanks to our first readers: Idrisa Pandit, Suvir Kaul, and Otoniya Juliane Okot Bitek.

Shukran jazilan and moteshakeram to:
Mohja Kahf, who makes it a necessity to think book-length thoughts.
Yasmine Abou-el-Kheir, generous friend and superhero librarian fairy godmother.
Khashayar Mohammadi, provider of Persian poetry via pink flamingo post, kindness itself.
Randeep Purewall, fellow inhabitant of borderless realms.
Niharika Pandit, Akshita Nagpal, Manahil Bandukwala, Sanna Wani, spreaders of *Cosmophilia*.
Marguerite Pigeon, Meredith Quartermain, and the original Rhizomatics. May we meet next year at Tamam, the liberated Palestine of East Van.

Gratitude to Suzanne Muir, Sarah Khan, Zehra Naqvi, and Kelty McKinnon.

Shukriyah and love to my mother and her siblings and our extended Kashmiri family and friends. Homage to the strength and courage of Kashmiri women. Shukriyah and love to Sumayya Syed and her family. Adaab and love to Reyhan Chaudhuri and Shadma Khatoon. Sehat aur salamat mein hamesha jeete raho.

Homage with garlands of roses and marigolds to the courageous Dehlavis, the women of Shaheen Bagh, movers of heaven and earth, defenders and uplifters of humanity. I couldn't be in Delhi, so I never actually met any of them, but they kept my spirit alive in what Sumayya would call that last heart-eating winter before the plague.

This book would not exist without the unwavering vision and support of my editor, Catriona Strang, and the sincerity and dedication of the Talonbooks publishing team.

—**RAHAT KURD**

SUMAYYA SYED is a poet, translator, and graduate student of sociology living in Kashmir. Her poems have appeared in the *Puritan*, *KashmirLit*, and the *Shoreline Review*.

RAHAT KURD is a poet, cultural critic, and editor living in Vancouver. Her first collection of poems, *Cosmophilia*, was published by Talonbooks in 2015.